Christopher D. Coleman

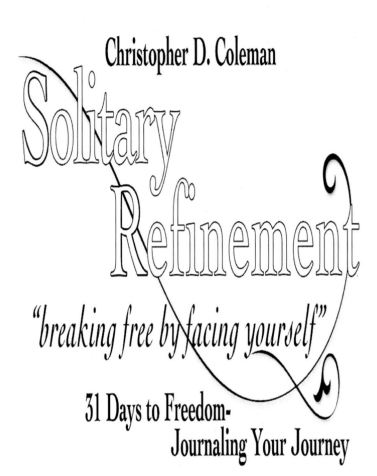

Solitary Refinement

"breaking free by facing yourself"

31 Days to Freedom-
Journaling Your Journey

To :

Welcome to what I hope to be the journey of your life. I am excited about the possibilities of you really opening up and digging in to a life changing experience. May your heart, mind, and soul be liberated.

_____

Christopher D. Coleman

Solitary Refinement

Copyright © 2008

Triumphant Encounters

Disclaimer: The purpose of this book is for general use only and is to aide in finding personal insight for each reader. It is not intended to replace professional counseling for emotional or psychological disorders or for any kind of treatment.

Scripture taken from the
NEW AMERICAN STANDARD BIBLE®, Copyright ©
1960, 1962, 1963, 1968, 1971, 1972, 1973, 1975,
1977, 1995 by The Lockman Foundation.
Used by permission.

Published by Triumphant Encounters, LLC
3509 Baker Rd. NW • Suite 403-174 • Acworth, GA 30101

ISBN: 978-0-615-24120-3

Printed in the United States of America

DEDICATION

I dedicate this book to my wonderful mother,
Linda C. Dunn, deceased brother, Marvin Coleman,
deceased friend, Christopher W. Tyler, and the son I know
God has for me, Zion Asher Coleman.

INTRODUCTION

From a wheelchair, I have observed people avoiding isues that I had to face. Those same people have watched me as I live my life from this chair, with a contorted body and a life span of rejection and abuse. They all have one question: "In your condition, how can you enjoy your life, when I am so miserable with mine?" The answer to the question is actually another question: "I have dealt with my disability; have you dealt with yours?" In other words, have you gotten alone with your mind, heart, and soul to correct, confront, and connect with who you are? This book is a journey through 31 issues a person cannot avoid and be truly content with themselves.

The heart, mind, and soul contain more information regarding who you are than your DNA. They are internal elements coming together to form your foundation. If these elements are not set on the same plane, the foundation will be cracked. A crack in our foundation allows peace to escape us. This results in psychomotor agitation – psychological and physical restlessness. Some people see this as a hole they need to fill with clay rather than a crack they need to seal with something that is concrete. When the storm of life comes and pours down on our foundation, which one do you think will weather the storm?

We need to feverishly deal with the broken pieces of our lives. It is nothing to be flippant about. A crack in our foundation is just as painful as a fractured bone. It too, needs attention. Leaving it unattended raises the risk of the crack becoming a complete break. Now is the time to tightly wrap the crack so it can grow back together.

Sealing this crack can only be done from the inside out. We must make our way down to the fragile places of our foundation; the spot where our heart, mind, and soul began to separate. Our traveling itinerary starts at the surface of our mind, goes deeper into the heart, and finally to the core of our soul. In order to do this, we will need to go through a process that will allow us to expose and analyze our minds, hearts, and souls. We have to go into the fractured places of our lives, pull our weakness out of darkness into the light, and observe what we see.

We must establish an introspective view of our foundation. The mind, heart, and soul must come together and assemble a fort around our peace while posing as a billboard that boldly states who we are. In this journey, we will analyze how the three internal elements interact with each other to form our foundation, and hopefully, bring them to a place of harmony. When these three are unified, you will become a stronger person.

Before you dive in, I want to make sure we are all on the same page. The first thing you need to know is that I will not give you the answer. Who am I to suggest that a certain method is the answer for your life? I don't know you personally well enough to do that. Nor will I ever know you that well. This book is simply to be used as a spotlight. I hope to shed some light in the deep and dark places of your inner being and hopefully, reveal to you what could be the answers for your situation. Nor am I going to sit here pretending to be this great philosopher and analyze every point for you. I'm going to encourage you to ask yourself, "Why does that hit me in the pit of my soul? What should I do with what this guy is saying?"

This journal is not an effort to explain some new pop-psychology theory, nor is it an attempt to convert you to a particular religious belief. Due to my knowledge, research, and belief in Christ, I do use psychological terms and quote the Bible. But at the end of the day, it is about the two of us discussing issues that will allow you to come face-to-face with yourself. So, for you, the non-believer, I want to challenge your narrow mindedness. Open yourself up to what I am saying. Christian, be real with yourself. Knowing who God is does not disqualify you from these issues. It just means you are supposed to have enough faith in Christ to allow Him to walk through these issues with you. And for everyone in between, I challenge you to spend the next 31 days right here in this book.

The Eve Of DAY 1

STOP **Did you read the Introduction? If not, why not? Go back and prepare yourself for all you will experience in the pages that follow.**

Ok. Are you ready now? Before tomorrow comes, it is very important for you to understand where I've been as the author and where I'm going with this book. When I was born, I was not breathing; therefore, pronounced dead. After 15 minutes of no oxygen to my brain, doctors were convinced that I would never move, walk, or talk. All of the repercussions of my birth meant that I would be a total vegetable for the rest of my life, imprisoned in a body of pain. At the time of writing this, I have lived a successful life with a disability known as Cerebral Palsy for 34 years. The method of really maximizing the life that I have here on earth has not been to deal with my external disability, but my internal disability. Whatever we deal with from within will change the outer for the better. I call this process 'weakness exposure.' Weakness exposure pulls things out of darkness and brings them to the light. This method helps us to see reality as it is.

I had to internally face what I thought about myself in my mind, how I felt about myself in my heart, and who I knew I was in the soul of my being. At that point, I stopped living my life in a wheelchair and started living from it. I realized that a wheelchair did not have the power to confine who I am. If I spent my whole life trying to do something that my disability did not allow me to do, it would be at that point I am confined. *We waste our whole lives trying to be what we are not because we refuse to understand who we are.* I could have exhausted myself fighting against my disability and never discovered my ability. This reality did not just pop up in my head; I had to grow to understand this concept. Knowing who I am inside was the exercise I needed to accomplish this external growth.

We waste our whole lives trying to be what we are not because we refuse to understand who we are.

Who I am now is no longer confined by my physical condition, even though it has not changed. I did not just jump out of my wheelchair one day and say, "I'm free." I grew out of it. My mind, heart, and soul have become stronger, causing my body to expand with the growth. You see, when something grows from the inside, the outer shell has to expand or it will break. My abilities have become the master over my disability. I graduated in the top five of my senior class. I moved on my own from Baton Rouge, Louisiana to Marietta, Georgia. I am the only one of a family of seven that went to and graduated from college. Finally, I am traveling all over the world motivating, challenging, and encouraging people to live a triumphant life.

It was when I started to develop my speaking career that I realized the issues I faced in the past were internal wheelchairs. These wheelchairs weren't exclusive to me due to my disability. We all have internal wheelchairs that can hinder our growth and potential. These internal wheelchairs play a vital role in our lives. This is why it's important to go through the next 31 days, one day at a time.

Did you notice that I did not put a table of contents in this book? Why not? Because I know you. You have a tendency to look at the chapters, pick out which ones apply to you, and possibly never read the rest of them. And then there are some of you who will read two or three chapters in one sitting, the same way you would read a novel.

Let me tell you both: You are missing out on what this book really has to offer you. As the author, I have been very strategic in the layout of each chapter. Each chapter builds upon itself. Do not… **DO NOT** rush through this process. Yes, each chapter is very short. But, if you really take in all that each chapter presents to you, it can very well be the longest book you will ever read. I'm going to encourage you to take your time and read each day, day-by-day. Really dig in and focus on what that day is saying to you.

Now, I'm no fool. I know that not everyone who picks up this book is going to have all 31 issues in their life. I also know this: Because this book builds upon itself, there are some procedures, concepts, and thoughts that you will need to have read in previous chapters before focusing on those days that uncover what you need for your life. In other words, each chapter prepares you for the next. Take your time. Read this book day-by-day. Answer the questions truthfully that are presented to you.

Because I am a professional keynote speaker, you might think this journal will be based on positive thinking. However, it is not. We will use reflective thinking rather than positive thinking because it requires us to operate in reality. Reflective thinking forces us to identify and define the problem, analyze the dilemma, come up with possible solutions, select the best answer, and finally, test and implement that resolution in our lives.

With this in mind, the first step of getting out of the wheelchair is admitting that you are in one, and coming to the point that you are ready to get out. That is the purpose of this journey. Make no doubt about it, this journal was written to shake up some things in you and bring you face-to-face with the reality of whatever wheelchair may be confining you.

⚠️Warning: The next 31 days will be a time to tear down, a time to restore, and a time to rebuild. I see you, the reader, as a diamond in the rough. I have written this journal to help you shave off your coarse characteristics and allow the brilliance of who you are to shine.

While reading this book, you'll probably say to yourself, "So-and-so needs to read this!" That may be true. But, it is also true that you are someone else's so-and-so, and they think you would benefit from what is in these pages, as well. Let me encourage you to start with yourself. Complete this journey before handing the book off to another. Gain some credibility by having the courage to break yourself free, first. What are the internal wheelchairs and fractured places in your life?

Correcting the MIND

DAY 1: Facing Your Mind

As a child, when I was awakened to the fact that I went from one room to another room on my knees while my siblings were able to walk there, my response was, "Only a dog moves around on all fours." That was my first taste of mental junk food. Over the next few years, I ate so much of it that I started regurgitating on myself. For example, when my siblings' friends would come over and look at me strangely because I was crawling, I would bark at them. I did this for two reasons. One reason was I wanted them to feel more afraid of me than they already were. But, two, I was uncomfortable with being on my knees and this was my way of dealing with it.

A thought in our minds is the first response to whatever life brings our way. Unfortunately, more often than not, this reply is identified as a Disconfirming Response. It is a response that causes a person to value him or herself as less. It is essential that we understand the mind to be the most treacherous tool we have because it can convince us to neglect our heart. This is dangerous since the mind validates what we see, hear, and feel. Most people operate in darkness rather than light because the mind will not permit them to separate facts from opinions. This forces us to deviate from the truth and acts of integrity.

The mind is the thought behind our emotions. Thoughts are seeds that take root in the heart and soul of man. When the heart and soul reject this invasion, Internal-Ego-Conflict begins to take place. Internal-Ego-Conflict occurs when the mind, heart, or soul become defensive because it feels it is being attacked. The mind can be the cause of frustration and destruction in one's life. This blunt element inflicts us with distress. We must get control over our mind or it will ruin us.

If you are living an oppressive, stressful life and you cannot move forward, it is because of the junk you have digested that is weighing heavily on your heart and soul. Follow me here. The mind is similar to the stomach. What you put into it affects everything, from your high blood pressure to your ability to think and reason. You need to be careful of your intake. Excuses and apathy are life's junk food. They weaken your mindset. You will not obtain real nourishment from them. The emptiness you are feeling will return very quickly.

Forget about excuses and apathy. Strengthen your state of mind instead. Take in things that will build you up, not make you feel like its okay to be complacent and sluggish. Feeling like this only creates the craving for a quick fix. We turn to motivational speakers, churches, and self-help books as if they are caffeine and energy drinks for the mind. What we are really doing is gaining weight. This intake only adds empty calories to the mind and makes us sicker with the person our minds say we are. It is time to go on a diet and allow the fatty cells of your mind to decrease.

Warning: There are some crude analogies below. I'm a writer, not a doctor who is going to talk to you in a bunch of technological terms. I am going to give it to you in layman's terms. You are sick, and I am going to be direct in my diagnosis.

YOUR MENTAL DIGESTIVE SYSTEM

Recognizing the mind as the stomach of life should make us cautious of not only what we eat, but also who is doing the cooking and serving the food. We want to believe we know so much about so many different areas and subjects; however, much of the source of our knowledge has come from eating out of a garbage can. We have embraced some thoughts and mindsets of some of the lowest forms of life. Yet, we wonder why we think the way we think about ourselves and other people. If you put garbage in, you shall get garbage out. To be frank with you, some of us need to take a mental enema. We need to flush out the garbage we have allowed into our minds. I know that hurts to hear, but sometimes pain is the only way to know how sick we really are.

We have to be careful with the things we allow our mind to recall. Once you swallow something and it comes back up, it is no longer food; it is vomit. Either it was too much for you to digest or it did not sit well on your stomach in the first place. Your mind cannot cope with what you are feeding it. Your mental digestive system is rejecting it for a reason. What looked to be good for you is actually spoiled. You can try to keep it in, but the mind will throw up on itself. All those things you keep bringing up are smelly, rotten, old garbage. You don't know this, so let me tell you: the people around you smell the vomit and they are gagging. Keep your mind focused on the fresh, nutritious, and natural things of life.

Your mind must be stimulated, not mutilated

The bottom line is this: your results are not supposed to have power over your thinking; your thinking is supposed to be in command of your results. In order to do this, *your mind must be stimulated, not mutilated.* To correct your mind is simply to give in to your heart and soul. The mind must accept and acknowledge your other internal elements within. It should respond to the truth that is in you. The good things we put into our mind will agree with and enhance who we are.

—— CORRECTING THE MIND ——

Who are you allowing to influence your thoughts?

If any, what types of books are you reading?

How fresh is the information?

Is there any nutritious value to what you are taking in?

What would people think about you, if you did speak your mind?

Discuss today's topic with other readers at
www.solitary-refinement.com.

A challenge from the Author:
There are organic foods for our minds.

Finally, brethren, whatever is true, whatever is honorable, whatever is right, whatever is pure, whatever is lovely, whatever is of good repute, if there is any excellence and if anything worthy of praise, dwell on these things.
~ Philippians 4:8 (NASB)

STOP Remember …

Read, meditate, and process just one day at a time.

Don't rush your journey.

DAY 2: Truth Is Not Best Sugarcoated

For about a year, I took a break from speaking and began to work for the church where I was a member at that time. My role was to plant a church in inner-city Atlanta near government-subsidized housing. Due to the fact that we did not have a location at the time, my team and I felt that it was crucial to start building relationships with the community and getting them acclimated to going to church. We started to bus about 25 adults and children from inner-city Atlanta to the church I was a part of, which happened to be a suburban, white church. In staff meetings every Monday, I would hear comments like, "Those kids are loud," as if the other teenagers weren't. Someone even threatened to call the police on one of the children for not paying for a 25¢ donut. Finally, after weeks and weeks of this reaction, the question was finally presented to me, "Are these kids comfortable outside of their environment?" What they were trying to get me to see all along is that they were not comfortable with having these kids brought into their environment. I believe if that had been said from the very beginning, we could have avoided a lot of confrontations and ill feelings.

With that in mind, I want to congratulate you and let you know how proud I am of you for picking up this book. Why? I know that the title alone will turn most people away. Who wants to spend 31 days dealing with themselves?

As a matter of fact, a friend of mine in marketing encouraged me to choose a different title. He said most people may not read this book simply because they don't want to deal with their internal issues. He suggested that I change the title and the presentation of the book. He believes that I can challenge the readers without being so straightforward and in-your-face. I thought to myself, "Why would I sugarcoat the truth?" Sugarcoating the truth will only stop the reader from identifying what they need in order to grow at this juncture of their lives.

Truth is processed energy that empowers the mind. When it is converted into power, your life will take off. The mind now has the power to develop concepts and opinions; to reflect and reason. However, with power comes responsibility. Truth requires us to approach life intelligently. Out of the mind must come some degree of intelligence, discernment, and worldview. Truth enables us to make an informed response to life. It is fuel used to produce progress and motion in our lives.

Now, with all of this in mind, do something for me. Take a cup of sugar and go dump it into the fuel tank of your car. What is the problem? Is it that sugar in gas does not just vaporize? In fact, when the gas heats up, the sugar in it breaks down just enough for the combination of the two to form a gritty syrup. This thick gooey mixture finds its way to the engine of your car. Wait, it gets better. After this mixture cools back down, it crystallizes and becomes a hardened part of the engine. You have ruined your car.

We do a similar thing to the mind when we sugarcoat the truth. Our attempt to make the truth more appealing may seem to be barely noticeable. However, if you look under the hood you will see you have a mess on your hands. Ambiguous approaches are bringing progress and motion to a halt. Sugarcoated truth has lessened the degree of intelligence, discernment, and worldview that can be brought to the table.

Anyone who intimidates others to the degree that they make others feel the need to sugarcoat the truth is the biggest and worst type of coward there is. Because, the truth is, you are not brave enough to take on the challenge of defeating the wimp within you. You don't want to accept the straight-out truth you need to become a better person.

PEAS IN THE POTATOES

It's a lot like putting sweet peas under a spoonful of mashed potatoes and then giving it to the baby. Some would say, "What is wrong with that? We are getting in the nutrition that the baby would not take in any other way." The problem is that when that baby grows up healthy and strong, he will think it was because of the creamy, buttery mashed potatoes; the one thing that will surely make him fat. He will not realize that it was the peas he needed all along. Sugarcoating the truth is the same principle. *We puff people up while sliding in a little truth, hoping they will take the bait. It's a known fact that all bait leads to bondage.* Songwriter Lauryn Hill once said, "People want fantasy, but what they need is reality." I agree with her. We need to stop validating one another's lives at any and all cost. We often say that the truth is not in a certain man or a woman. I would have to argue with that

We puff people up while sliding in a little truth, hoping they will take the bait. It's a known fact that all bait leads to bondage.

statement. Any person that has the ability to think and reason possesses the truth within them. They just choose not to acknowledge it.

The truth is the most valuable and powerful thing we can ever possess on earth. It is said that the best things for us are pure. With these two thoughts in mind, why would we not want the pure truth in our lives? In order to really face all that this book will present, you must put on something I call a Truth Filter. A Truth Filter is a strainer on our hearts, minds, and souls that separates facts from opinions. It allows us to operate in light rather than darkness.

Sugarcoating the truth will surely prove to be an ineffective method. We have to tell ourselves, and others, that those peas are good for you. Now shut your trap and eat them as-is. I will not hide the peas under the mashed potatoes for you in the remainder of this book. However, I will make every effort to uncover and enlighten the truth you need in order to grow. Ultimately, the choice to accept and feed off this truth will be yours.

——— CORRECTING THE MIND ———

Are you the big baby that is gagging from the taste of truth and making your friends feel like they have to sugarcoat it?

Are you the parent that is trying to slip the peas in under the mashed potatoes instead of being frank with yourself and your friends?

What do you need to say or hear to acknowledge pure truth?

Discuss today's topic with other readers at
www.solitary-refinement.com.

A challenge from the Author:
A person that sugarcoats truth for others
lies to himself.

I have not written to you
because you do not know the truth,
but because you do know it, and because no lie
is of the truth. ~ 1 John 2:21 (NASB)

STOP Remember ...
Read, meditate, and process just one day at a time.
Don't rush your journey.

DAY 3: Falling Apart & Don't Have it Together

After graduating from college, I knew that going back to Louisiana would ultimately mean that I would have to give up on any hope for my independence. So, I decided not to move back to Baton Rouge, but build a life in Marietta, Georgia. That decision meant that I had to become totally responsible for my well-being and find a way to support myself. I found myself without a job and receiving Social Security Income of $600 a month for the first three and a half years. Thank God, my landlord was a good friend of mine who month-after-month allowed me to stay there without paying rent. However, I still had to feed and clothe myself, pay credit card debt, and student loans, all on $600 a month. Believe it or not, it wasn't the situation that was destroying me; it was my conduct in the middle of the situation that almost sabotaged my life.

Five, four, three, two, one... Showtime! This is the way we live our lives day-in and day-out. We have this way of thinking that the moment we step foot outside the front door, we are now on center stage. It's time to put on a fake smile, act out the phony attitude, and put on a show for everybody. We do this because we yearn for everyone to accept us for who we want them to think we are.

How long do you intend to play this 24/7 game of charades? Do you not know you stink at it? You have everyone fooled except the most important person: you. You can act out whatever you want to in your mind - your heart and soul know better. *Affirmation does not come by pretending to be who you desire to be. It is your ability to be who you are that validates you.*

Let me introduce you to a new concept called Inter-Debunk. Inter-Debunk happens when everything in you comes out and exposes who you really are. You begin to fall apart because you cannot take losing in this game of charades. The mental masquerade is not working and you are not able to deal with it. You are not breaking down because life is too much. That's right; the fact is, you got your feathers ruffled because life is questioning your character and digging up what you tried to bury - and you don't like it. My picture is on the back of the book, so go ahead and slap my face; I know

Affirmation does not come by pretending to be who you desire to be. It is your ability to be who you are that validates you.

you want to. That doesn't change what I am saying here. It is time for you to stop avoiding who you are. It is called Defensive Communication, a behavior that arises in a person when they feel the need to protect themselves.

There is something interesting about all of this. The same people we are putting on a show for, are putting on a show for us! They are putting on a show to make us think that we have to put on a show for them. You see, we all live in this world of hurt, regret, fears, and doubts. These are four unavoidable elements of life. These elements do not shy away from a person because of educational levels, social status, financial position, race, or gender.

THE SHOW MUST NOT GO ON

Every day you get up on that stage is another day you have to get off. Another day you have to go home and pump yourself up all over again for tomorrow. Another day of trying to convince yourself that you are not tired of faking it and this routine is not getting old. But you are tired of faking it, are you not? This routine is getting old to you. And you don't know how long you can go on with the show.

Each time you get back up on that stage, dancing and prancing around, you shake up those elements of your life.

Just like a soda-pop can when you shake it up and the elements inside get mixed together, a chemical reaction starts and eventually causes an explosion. If you don't pop the cap yourself, you will break down in the middle of the act while everyone is watching. Let's be honest. Isn't this one of your biggest fears? That one day in the middle of the show it will all come crumbling down for the world to see that you don't have it all together?

How about breaking down now, in your living room with no one watching you. Just say it, "I hurt. I regret so many things. I have my doubts. I am afraid. I am so uncertain about my future. I don't have things together the way I want everyone to think I do." Don't live a mirage life. What good is a life filled with illusions? We all deserve to have a life of substance. Reality is the key that opens the door to that life.

—— CORRECTING THE MIND ——

What are your most painful hurts?

What are your deepest regrets?

What are your doubts?

What are you afraid of?

Discuss today's topic with other readers at
www.solitary-refinement.com.

A challenge from the Author:
Have you ever felt, deep down inside of you,
a calm in the middle of life's storms?

Be anxious for nothing, but in everything by prayer and supplication with thanksgiving let your requests be made known to God. And the peace of God, which surpasses all comprehension, will guard your hearts and your minds in Christ Jesus. ~ Philippians 4:6-7 (NASB)

STOP Remember …

Read, meditate, and process just one day at a time.

Don't rush your journey.

DAY 4: Foolish Ways VS. Gained Wisdom

I'm going to tell you the truth. Right now I don't want to be transparent for two reasons. One is my pride. Two, I know my mom is reading this book. And, for the next 25 years she is going to say, "I told you so." Nevertheless, here it goes. Moving off campus into my own apartment before graduating was a foolish decision on my part. My deceased brother, Marvin, had always played a very supportive role in my life. From going to high school to deciding to move from Baton Rouge to Marietta, Marvin was the one who said, "Go for it." But, when I called him and told him I wanted to move off campus and into my own place, I did not listen to what he was trying to tell me. All I heard was, "Don't do it." So, I did it. I did not understand that my 3.1 was not going to go to work for me and pay the bills I was accumulating. I started living off student loans; in my case, stupid loans. I also wasn't looking at the fact that credit cards were not paying the bills; they were deferring the bills and adding more interest to them. I wish I had known that the method to my madness would eventually lead me down the wrong road. I refused to see what my brother wanted me to see.

Usually I encourage everyone to read each day, but if you are 25 years old or younger, you may not be ready to accept what I am going to say. You are foolish if your method for life is not based on the logic from experience. Wisdom comes through the test of time, no exceptions. Unless they are mentally ill or letting issues affect their ability to reason, the wisest person in the room is most often the oldest person in the room. A person that is gaining wisdom accepts this.

Wisdom is effective application of knowledge and experience gained through the years. It is applying experienced logic to life. Make no mistake; there is nothing wrong with trial and error. We can have a good theory on life. However, we must recognize this theory as untested logic; that is hypothetical reasoning that is not mature enough to be considered logic on which to base life.

To really begin to increase wisdom, the mind must be willing to do some reverse brainstorming. In your mind, you must collect a list of ideas or solutions that would make the problem worse. After generating such a list, consider the implications of doing the opposite of what was identified. It is essential to be able to scrutinize the mind. It is very important to investigate your thinking and its outcome.

MISTAKING INTELLIGENCE FOR WISDOM

The best part about being 30 something is the ability to glance back into my 20's and recognize how much good judgment I did not have and how much is still lacking. I could have sworn I was acquainted with all I needed to know to live the way I thought I wanted to live. I was mistaking intelligence for wisdom. Now I ask myself, "How many times did my mom bite her tongue and say, 'That is a lesson that he will only learn through life. No matter what I say, he will not listen simply because it is coming from me.'" Today, I would rather be an old man with wisdom, than a young man with knowledge.

Because of my disability and what I had to go through, you could say I am a little wiser than someone else my age, but I am certainly not where I could be if I had used experienced logic. Now I know wisdom comes from the experiences you go through in life. Until a method is tested, it is not proven to work. As young people, we build our life for this moment in time. We fail to look toward the future. We must understand that a quick solution is a temporary fix. Real answers are not temporary fixes. Young people live for the moment. Old people live in the past. Wise people look toward the future.

The wisest thing you can ever do is to understand your level of stupidity.

The wisest thing you can ever do is to understand your level of stupidity. You need to know the limits of your understanding and knowledge. A wise person opens their thinking to the possibility that they are not seeing the whole picture. Our eyes cannot see any more than what we are focused on at the time. The closer you are to the situation, the less visibility you have to see the full picture. The key here is a venerable person or sage. This is a person of age with impressive dignity and profound wisdom. This is why it is essential to have a teachable spirit. Stupidity comes into play when you and I do not listen to people standing in the background. Because they are farther away from the picture, they can whisper nuggets of truth in our ears that will broaden our perspective. Understanding this has made me wiser.

—— CORRECTING THE MIND ——

Steps to acquiring wisdom:

You are going to ask your friends their thoughts anyway; limit it to only three of your most mature friends.

Would you want your child to feel like they can come to you for advice? Give your parents that same opportunity.

Find a man and a woman that are 10, 20, and 30 years older than you to be your advisors.

Discuss today's topic with other readers at
www.solitary-refinement.com.

A challenge from the Author:
Wisdom enhances our thinking while
challenging our conduct.

...How long, O naive ones, will you love being simple-minded? And scoffers delight themselves in scoffing And fools hate knowledge? ~ Proverbs 1:22 (NASB)

 Remember ...

Read, meditate, and process just one day at a time.

Don't rush your journey.

DAY 5: Dealing with No Progress

I built my speaking career on the analogy of getting out of my wheelchair. I tell my audience that we all have some type of wheelchair in our lives, but we don't have to be confined. Most people think my wheelchair is only the combination of the wheels and metal pieces they see on the stage. However, I, too, have other wheelchairs, as well. My entire life has always been one fight after another fight to get to the next level. Whatever I was trying to accomplish, there was always someone there, not only to tell me I could not do it, but to put obstacles in my way to prove their point. I don't mind telling you that I don't think it is right that I have to deal with my disability on top of fighting against negative people to do what I know I can do. The opinions of others should not be a barrier for me to reach my potential. However, the truth of the matter is that whatever is in me that makes me not want to fight back has the potential to be my wheelchair. I have to ask myself, "What is truly holding me back?"

Many of us look in the mirror and put a face to the rut we are stuck in. If that doesn't leave a sickly feeling deep down inside of you, that statement wasn't as audible as I would have liked for it to be. So let me repeat it: Many of us look in the mirror and put a face to the rut we are stuck in.

Now, you are probably saying, "Whoa whoa whoa, back it up! That's a very sensitive subject for you to bring up right now." To tell you the truth, this is a subject that I would not even consider tackling except for the fact that we blame the rut on someone else. We actually think that there is some other reason than our own selves that make us immovable, confined to this rut in the road of life.

Here is reality: If you are above the age of 18 and have the mental capacity to pick up this book and read it to yourself, then there is no one you can blame for this condition you have chosen to live in day after day. Letting your present condition be the deciding factor of your future is the basis for your rut.

If you look up the definition of the word "rut" in the American Heritage Concise Dictionary, you will find that a rut is a sunken track or groove made by a *driver* of a vehicle. Now, can I call your attention to the fact that it was made by a driver of the vehicle? That's you and me. We have each made our own ruts. And, I'm here to tell you that our self-made ruts are caused by one or some combination of three things: complacency, laziness and self-pity.

Now is the time to evaluate the influence our mind has over our life. When the mind defines the self-worth of a person, they are either vain or have a very low self-esteem. There is nothing in the world that can have a stronger grip on us than our minds. By the way, I am in a wheelchair as I write this. Between the mind, heart, and soul, the mind is the only one that tolerates complacency, laziness, or self-pity.

COMPLACENCY

We get to a place in our lives where we feel we no longer have to strive for progress. For some reason, we think we can just coast when we get to a certain level. We believe from that point forward we will be able to maintain that position or drift our way to the top. Here are two factors that prove why that method will never work: gravity and wind. If we are not watchful, we will be blown into places we didn't want to go or pushed back to the position we worked so hard to get away from. The truth is that it will take effort to maintain that position and even more effort to travel beyond it. We have to apply effort no matter where we are in our lives in order to stay where we are or to experience progress.

Complacency is our way of cheating ourselves. We don't want to give ourselves the time or the effort we know we need in order to mature to the next juncture of our lives. We settle for less than the best, not because we can't get the best, but because we don't want to put forth the work that is required for growth.

We have to ask ourselves who we are really hurting by that mindset. The one who says, "Finally, I have arrived!" is the one who admits their reason for living ceases to exist. Now what? Once you get to the place in your life when you feel you have accomplished everything and have done everything there is to do, you put yourself back in the same boat with the person that has accomplished and done nothing. Yet, we wonder why we have this empty feeling in the pit of our soul.

LAZINESS

Laziness is literally a lack of commitment to yourself. You don't want to do what needs to be done in order to reach the growth you know you can achieve. You will never even reach the point of complacency because it requires too much to get there in the first place.

⚠ Warning: A lazy man never leaves footprints in the sand for someone to follow. If you say, "I can't" before you try, you are not incapable; you are lazy. The idea of not finding out if you can or cannot do something is your way of not having someone requiring something from you. "If they don't know I can do it, they won't ask me to do it." That is just the most immature and slothful way to approach life.

Opportunity after opportunity has passed us by because of sluggishness. Sure, we would like to say we were just being patient, waiting for the right opportunity. But the truth is, we would not reach out for it and do the work to seize the moment. Laziness is not to be mistaken for patience. Patience is waiting for the occasion to do something, while laziness is not taking the initiative to do something.

Laziness in a person is a physical demonstration of his or her mind. The mind trains the body. So, if the body is weak, it's a reflection of a weak mind. This person physically puts off today, while mentally knowing they will not do it tomorrow. They rely on luck rather than acting on hope. In return, they open the door and windows of their life for regrets to come in.

SELF-PITY

At the time of writing this book, I have lived 34 years in a wheelchair. To be totally frank with you, self-pity is not something I tolerate. Therefore, this session will be short, but it will not be sweet. It will probably be one of the most direct and to-the-point pieces of literature you will ever read.

Self-pity is a well-masked, undercover form of pride. You actually think your situation, your problems, and your circumstances are so much worse than the next person's. You believe you have a right to complain. You think you have an excuse to be lazy and complacent. *Sounds of Blackness* wrote a song I recommend to you. It is called "Back to Life, Back to Reality."

Let me tell you the number-one issue that I have with self-pity. Self-pity is the core; that is, the foundation, of all addiction. Take a moment and let that sink in: *Self-pity is the core – the foundation – of all addiction.* The reason we run to substance abuse and other addictive things is because we do not feel we are getting the adequate response to our current situations. "Life is so difficult that I have to have this thing to cope." Before, it was just something to smooth over the situation, but now it's something that you can't live without. And it's all in view of the fact

Self-pity is the core – the foundation – of all addiction.

that you felt like the world owed you something. This life isn't fair to you. Congratulations, you bought into your own hogwash.

Don't let your mind lead you to an impasse. Break loose from the thinking that tells you this is all there is to life. You must become a cultist person. That is, you must have the highest level of devotion to progress in your life. It is time to stop holding yourself back mentally.

—— CORRECTING THE MIND ——

Identify your rut: A. Complacency   B. Laziness
                       C. Self-pity   D. All of the above

Into what area of your life do you need to put more effort?

List 5 things:
A. You need to do…
B. You should do…
C. You want to do…

If you complete these things, how would it change you and your relationships?

Be real with yourself: On a scale from one to ten, how big are your problems compared to the rest of the world?

Discuss today's topic with other readers at www.solitary-refinement.com.

A challenge from the Author:
A life without progress is the result of
an undisciplined life.

For even when we were with you, we used to give you this order: if anyone is not willing to work, then he is not to eat, either. For we hear that some among you are leading an undisciplined life, doing no work at all, but acting like busybodies. ~2 Thessalonians 3:10-11 (NASB)

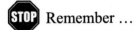 Remember …
Read, meditate, and process just one day at a time.
Don't rush your journey.

DAY 6: Failures to Reach Victory

Every day so far, I have tried to give you examples of how each issue applies to my life. Today you could say I'm going to fail at that. I do not have an example of failure. Not because I have not made a bunch of mistakes. Believe me; I have. It is because I am not dead. Every breath I take is another opportunity to use those mistakes to enhance, grow, and educate myself. A person can make a mistake on a test without failing it. Therefore, I believe failure for you and me is to come to the end of our lives and not be a better person because of our mistakes.

We have to stop looking for excuses to explain our defeats and face up to them. It is time to take advantage of the learning curve between losing and winning. This curve is our chance to observe life, learn from life, and grow in life. Victory and failure depend on your ability to see who you are. The mind only sees things as black or white, yes or no, success or defeat. This bipolar mindset is hindering us from observing, learning, and growing. Going from one extreme to another does not open the door for us to face opposition.

Opposition in one's life is necessary for victory.

The process of overcoming failure is victory. This process requires perseverance, endurance, pursuit of desires, and confrontation of challenges. Since this is the case, the only things that make a failure a failure instead of a learning and growing observation, are pride and laziness. There is such a thing as successful-failure. Successful-failures are let-downs that make us realize our potential for success. *The decision to get up from a fall transforms a bad start into an amazing finish.*

The decision to get up from a fall transforms a bad start into an amazing finish.

Success through the observation of failure is priceless. The ability to study your life and arrive at a conclusion that changes you for the better is ground-breaking in any situation. Discontentment reveals your need for progress. It is an evaluation of where you are. Every test we fail in life is only a practice test, if we learn from it. This trial lets us know the areas that need improvement. We cannot pass a test we have not prepared for. Every small test, even if we do not pass it, prepares us for a bigger test. In our efforts to correct our mistakes, we discover our aptitude.

STOP IT!

Failure should not stop you; you should stop it. When you really learn from your experiences, you will master your mistakes. Failure that informs you gives you control of your situation. Victory is not measured by what a person accomplishes, but by the overwhelming odds they take on with courage. Trials give accomplishments their value. A Japanese saying is, "Failure teaches success."

Through your failures, you have an opportunity to grow and further develop as a person. Maturing in the difficult times is victory. If you do something that is immediately successful, it's not victory. Victory comes through trial and error. Overnight success is only overnight because you have not had the opportunity to grow. You must develop determination. The difference between the impossible and the possible lies within a person who possesses determination. Determination conquers every failure. If you allow it, failure is that best friend that pushes you to the next level. Zig Ziglar once said, "Learning how to benefit from your failure is the secret to success."

As I said before, failure presents an opportunity to gain knowledge from your errors. The person that does not take this opportunity is not a failure, but a coward. Learning from your mistakes is victory!

Finally, your opinion about yourself is a key factor in success or failure. Your success is not found in someone else's actions. It is found first in yours. The only power on earth strong enough to keep you from succeeding is you. It's a mindset. It's answering the question, "Who do I want to be as an individual?" A conqueror is born when they believe they can defeat an adversary and win the fight.

——— CORRECTING THE MIND ———

Admit where you are.
Visualize where you can be.
GO THERE.

Discuss today's topic with other readers at
www.solitary-refinement.com.

A challenge from the Author:
A conqueror seeks victories through their failures.

These things I have spoken to you, so that in Me you may have peace. In the world you have tribulation, but take courage; I have overcome the world.
John 16:33 (NASB)

 Remember ...
Read, meditate, and process just one day at a time.
Don't rush your journey.

DAY 7: Live with Regrets or Make a Change

Up until a couple of days ago I had a hard time thinking of something I would share with you as my regret. But, yesterday, someone said something to me. Not to hurt me or make me feel bad, but to challenge and encourage me to do better. But, what I replayed in my mind was, "You are not good enough." Not only did I hear that, but I heard every negative comment that was said through my whole life. Now, I can tell you my regret. I regret the things that I allow to infiltrate my mind. In this instance, I'm not talking about movies, the TV, or other tabloids. I'm talking about the verbal and non-verbal communication of doctors, therapists, psychologists, and, yes, even some of my own friends and family. Now, you say, "That's fine, Chris. But, most people would look at the mistakes that they have made as their regrets." Let me tell you what I have learned about my own mistakes. Ninety-five percent of them have been the result of what was going on in my mind. I have let people's thoughts and opinions define who I am. Here's the kicker. I have come to realize that the hardest thing to change is your mind about yourself. This is the reason why so many of us live with regrets.

Now, when I talk about regret I don't mean the type of regret that comes from selling a car or seeing a bad movie. I am talking about life-altering disappointments. Regret is your action or lack of action that negatively changes your perspective on life. It is mourning over a situation that could or should be different. Grieving over a situation is detrimental. There is a point where your grief becomes a mental harm. Most people mourn over death because it is indefinite. Mourning something that has the ability to endure is devaluing your life. Regret is the choice not to be transformed. We mentally choose to live life disappointed.

Your regrets are oftentimes your justification for not living a significant life.

If your life has been enhanced, clarified, or even simplified by change through a tough situation, you should have no regrets. If you do have misgivings, it is because you have not opened yourself to experiencing the growth of a change. Lamenting is a premeditated emotion; an emotion that we think through and decide to embrace.

Your regrets are oftentimes your justification for not living a significant life. You cannot afford to waste life reflecting on what you cannot redo. You must remove the weight of the past from yourself.

Regret can be a crippling emotion. Embracing something to the degree that it makes you motionless is dangerous. This is what we are going to talk about today; those danger zones that we encounter through our lack of motion.

DANGER ZONE 1: SPILLED MILK

Regret is our way of diplomatically reminding ourselves of the things we've done wrong. It is not accepting the fact that what is done is done. It is a self-inflicted trap used to confine us. It is the decision to hold yourself captive for your mistakes. That's right. Regret is bondage! It is our mental effort to punish ourselves. I remember a friend of mine who had a little two-year-old daughter. My friend went into the living room of her house and found the little girl standing in the corner. She asked her daughter why she was putting herself in timeout. That is exactly what we do when we choose to hold on to regrets. We choose to put ourselves in the corner even though we have the freedom to move forward with our lives.

DANGER ZONE 2: GUILT

Facing your regrets is not about feeling guilty or wishing you could do it all over again. "If I could do it all over again" is a nice thought, but the fact is, we can't do it all over again. Moments in time cannot be relived, only rectified. You can't take back what you said. You can't react the scene. You can't rebuild the bridges that you burned. You cannot go back there.

I remember in math class after we would take a test, the teacher would go back over every problem that was on that test. This was not so that we could take it over again. The grade we received would not be changed. However, math builds upon itself. What we have to realize is that we can't take that test over and redo all those mistakes; *but another test is coming*. It may be harder than the previous one. We will have to apply all we have learned when it's time for the next test.

DANGER ZONE 3: HYPOCRISY

A person who forgives another, yet is still being influenced by their regrets, is a hypocrite. At this point, lamenting is the fear of holding yourself accountable for making a change. A change starts when you accept the responsibility for where you are. It requires you to do what is right over what is wrong, even when you don't feel like it. It means giving up the excuse you use to stay where you are, do what you have been doing, and be the way you want to be. It is the decision to move forward.

For some reason, we think that simply saying, "I regret that" automatically gives us compassion for the situation. Therefore, we are saying it's okay to be in that situation. Regret becomes our excuse in life. Instead of using it as an excuse, we need to learn from the situation and do something different, or even better, than before.

A regret could be not saying something you know you should have said. As the author, I don't want to live with regrets, either. You can understand that, right? So, let me just go ahead and say it. Stop wallowing in your past, get off your butt, and move on with your life.

—— CORRECTING THE MIND ——

In what corner are you remaining?

What can you learn from your past?

What can you do differently now?

What needs to be done in your life for you to stop turning your regrets into excuses?

Discuss today's topic with other readers at
www.solitary-refinement.com.

A challenge from the Author:
The Bible does not have the word regret in it,
but it does have the name Redeemer.

Let the words of my mouth and the meditation of my heart.
Be acceptable in Your sight, O Lord, my rock and
my Redeemer. ~ Psalm 19:14 (NASB)

 Remember …
Read, meditate, and process just one day at a time.
Don't rush your journey.

DAY 8: Fears and Doubts

Is it possible to live life without fears and doubts? I would like to say, the one who lives without them is not taking responsibility for their own life. However, the truth is that not taking responsibility is a result of fears and doubts. I don't care who you are; you have doubts and fears. The big, the strong, and the athletic have misgivings and worries. The rich, the intellectual, and the powerful have theirs, too. Now you say, what about the brave? A brave person is not one without doubts and fears. A brave person is one who acknowledges they have them and chooses to take them on.

There is no way around them. It is not only okay, it is natural for us to have chronic fears and doubts. This is when the mind plays games with us. The mind cannot control what is natural. So it makes us think what is natural is wrong and what is unnatural is justifiable. We think any signs of weakness must be concealed rather than exposed. Exposing our weaknesses helps us see the reality of our life. We want to believe it is natural to conceal them because it protects us from external harm. What about internal harm? When we shut in our fears and doubts, something happens deep inside of us.

It is not natural to walk the floors at night. It is not normal to think someone is waiting to get you at every corner you turn. It is unnatural to justify broken dreams. Who lives life to the fullest without having goals? You are supposed to enjoy life. You should not worry about your kids so much that you do not let them out of your sight. All of this is the outcome of hiding your doubts and fears. I'm sorry, but that type of life is not natural. I don't care what you tell yourself in your mind. A lot of people we think are crazy are not; they just decided not to deal with the fears and doubts of life. You are not having a breakdown; you are at a crossroad. You must decide if you are going to face your fears and doubts or run from them. Your mind may tell you it is okay to walk away. Why? Because oftentimes facing fears and doubts requires us to do something the mind can't conceive.

I remember the summer I convinced my mom that in spite of my dependence on a wheelchair for mobility, I should move from Baton Rouge, Louisiana to Marietta, Georgia to attend Southern Polytechnic State University. Everybody thought that I had no doubts or fears with this move. Everybody thought that Christopher knew exactly what was in front of him. Nevertheless, the moment they shut the door and left me in that dormitory by myself, I broke down. I was overwhelmed with uncertainty.

You know what? Some of those very doubts and fears became my reality. But now I know it is okay to walk in darkness when you are headed to the light. The reality of some of my biggest concerns convinced me that I could overcome anything. I tell you this because I do not want you to think I am trying to down-play the subject. I am not. However, in the years since moving to Georgia in 1995, my life has changed. The fears and doubts that I once had no longer exist. Instead, they are more complex. But, I'm not intimidated by them like most.

FAITH OR STUPIDITY?

We cannot let doubts and fears intimidate us. Life cannot be fully experienced with a timid approach to uncertainty. We must investigate doubts and fears before we allow them to influence us. How in the world do we do this? We need to determine whether or not they are merely caution signs or warning signs. A caution sign means, "Be careful how you approach things." A warning sign means, "I would not go there if I were you."

Let's start by first dealing with caution. Caution simply means to be responsible for your actions. A lot of times, doubts and fears only enter our minds to make us aware of the *possible* outcome. **Note:** I said possible outcome, not definite outcome. It means that if you do it this way, this very well could be the consequence. It is a chance to make a shift toward our desired destination.

Warning means to be aware of the outcome. Someone often warns you of something because they have been there, done that, and they don't believe you are going to want the same results. Warnings in your life are nothing to fool around with. They signify that danger is in the area. Now, I'm going to be truthful with you. Just because a fire alarm goes off doesn't mean there is a fire in the building, but if it were me I would get out and assess the situation. There must be a long and detailed evaluation of our hesitation. We have to take a step outside of the situation and look at it from multiple angles before moving forward. Like my mom would say, "Don't be a fool."

But, we need to be careful not to put faith in our stupidity.

The secret to facing our doubts and fears is to know if they are simply warning signs or caution signs. So how do we know? Like I said, it is simple. Does the situation require faith or stupidity? There is a line to be drawn there. Faith is to see both sides and believe; whereas, stupidity is to ignore the warning signs. *But, we need to be careful not to put faith in our stupidity.*

Lately, during the question and answer times after my lectures, the most common asked question has been, "What is your greatest fear?" I tell them that my greatest fear is one day waking up at 80 years old on my deathbed and realizing that I let my wheelchair stop me from living the life that had been granted to me. Can I get into your space for a moment? Your greatest fear should be letting something you cannot control, control you. Believing you can somehow change a situation by crying, arguing, and complaining about it is not faith; it is stupidity.

—— CORRECTING THE MIND ——

Are you facing a caution or a warning sign?

Will you regret taking that step more than not taking it?

Why or why not?

Are you being faithful or stupid?

Discuss today's topic with other readers at
www.solitary-refinement.com.

A challenge from the Author:
The secret to overcoming fears and
doubts requires a person to receive
power, love and discipline.

For God has not given us a spirit of timidity, but of power
and love and discipline. ~ 2 Timothy 1:7 (NASB)

STOP Remember …
Read, meditate, and process just one day at a time.
Don't rush your journey.

DAY 9: Where You Have Been & Where You Are

Writing this book has forced me to go down memory lane. It has made me recall some of my decisions, made me look at some of my results, and helped me to understand the consequences of where I am now. To tell you the truth, I am a better man because of this. I was awakened, through this book, to my own mistakes and consequences of life. I want to give you that same opportunity.

To be honest, I know that this day may be boring and a bit redundant for you. You may get halfway through this day and decide to skip it. Let me ask you this: Would you not say that there are points in our lives, like this, where we get bored and impatient, causing us to make wrong decisions in our lives? I want to encourage you to walk through this process of analyzing your decision-making method.

Many people often ask themselves this question: "How did I get here?" But for some reason, they never go any farther than that. The mind doesn't want to recall what we are asking it to remember. Can I just throw a question out there for you? Could it be that you don't want to face your past decisions because you don't want to be responsible for the future? In order to understand where we are, we must go mentally deeper. We must look at our history. The purpose of history is to learn from our mistakes and repeat our success. History aids us in analyzing the past, embracing the present, and visualizing the future.

The secret to understanding our history is one sim-ple equation. The equation is:

$$Decisions + Results = Consequences$$

Back to the question at hand: "How did we get here?" *The mind makes the decision, marginalizes the result, and minimizes the consequence.* Our decisions and the results of those decisions are the cornerstones of where we are today. We are at this point in our lives because of the decisions we have made. Our Decision-Making Methods are oftentimes similar to our spending habits and have some of the same results.

The mind makes the decision, marginalizes the result, and minimizes the consequence.

DECISION MAKING PROCESSES

Long-Term Decisions - Decisions that are affecting our lives over a wide span of time.

Short-Term Decisions - Choices that we are making that will affect the present and the near future.

No-Options Decisions - Choices forcing us to live in the outcome.

Spend-Now Decisions - Decisions we have to make whether we want to or not.

Investment Decisions - Choices we are making based upon the type of future we desire.

RESULTS OF DECISIONS

Mentally Bankrupt - Invested all of your emotions into a decision with no return.

Depleted Options - Continuing to make decisions one after another in order to rectify the previous decisions.

Bounced - Commitments and promises that our previous decisions will not allow us to follow up.

Emotional Investments (Good or Bad) - Decisions made based on vision for the future.

Options - Emotional Investments that have produced flexibility.

Debt – Decisions that have turned into dictators in our lives. At some point we all have to make the following Life-Molding Decisions. Using the above definitions, consider your decision making habits and evaluate your results:

Education: What level of ability, character, intelligence, and contribution do you want to bring to the table of your life?

Relationship: Who are you allowing to take up your time, influence your life, request your attention, and provoke your emotions?

Occupation: What activity have you chosen to occupy your time while receiving the income needed to support your desired lifestyle?

Spouse: With whom did you commit to living your life?

Spiritual Belief: Who do you ultimately believe controls the universe, and therefore dictates your outlook on life?

Lifestyle: What things are you surrounding yourself with and how do they define who you are?

Integrity: When have you decided to tell a lie instead of dealing with the truth?

The Reality of Your World: When have you chosen to accept the truth no matter how hard it was?

Excuses: What will you do to validate yourself?

Finances: How have you decided to spend your income?

Image: What impression do you want to leave on people?

—— CORRECTING THE MIND ——

What are the consequences?

Due to the methods and results of each decision, sum up the impact it has made on your life.

Discuss today's topic with other readers at

www.solitary-refinement.com.

A challenge from the Author:
Making decisions with your mind
and never consulting your heart and soul
will get in the way of
the will of God for your life.

And just as they did not see fit to acknowledge God any
longer, God gave them over to a depraved mind, to do those
things which are not proper... ~ Romans 1:28 (NASB)

 Remember ...
Read, meditate, and process just one day at a time.
Don't rush your journey.

DAY 10: Where You Are & Where You're Going

On my 30th birthday, I woke up different. I don't know what happened. It was like a light just went off inside of me. My thought was, "Time is wasting away and I need to get my act together." I analyzed every day for the last ten years of my life. I realized that at 30 years of age I had no savings, I was thousands of dollars in debt, I did not have a car, and lived in the basement of someone else's home. After that evaluation, I understood where I was, but was not content with where I was going. The decisions I made thus far were not going to give me the results I desired.

Congratulations! You made it! Yes, you have made some bad decisions, and the results of these decisions have impacted your life. But, you have made it this far. I believe 90% of the people all over the world would never get to the point where they face their decisions and accept their results. Most people would never move on with their lives because of this.

So, go ahead behind that closed door, and cry in unbelief and relief. For you who are too manly to cry, go ahead and punch the hell out of that wall. You know, the funny part is that some of the women are going to be the ones to punch the hell out of the wall, and some of the men are going to close the door and cry. But that's okay, too. Now some of you who know me personally are going to get your feathers in a ruffle because I used the word "hell". I say to you, "Chill Out!" This is a book that deals with real people and real issues. And to be real with you, we all feel like punching the hell out of a wall sometimes.

The relief you are feeling is a breakthrough. Breakthrough happens in every aspect of life. It snaps the chokehold that life sometimes has on us. A breakthrough experience teaches us to take on adversity and come back better than before. It is a phenomenon that strikes you in the pit of your soul. You will find yourself launched onto a higher plane of life. However, after the most awesome breakthroughs, the most crippling setbacks can take place and begin to threaten growth. No matter how much progress an individual makes, old behavior patterns will always try to prevail.

LIFE IS A TUG-OF-WAR

There will always be something in life that holds us back and pulls us ahead. Life is a tug-of-war. The side that wins is the same side on which we choose to place our focus. Your actions are not determined by your circumstances. They are determined by how you perceive your situation. You can never permit conditions, circumstances, or obstacles, regardless of their nature, to cause you to stop, back up, or ever slow down. This is the point you have to look at where you are and find inspiration to move forward. There are two things you must have in order to get to the next level: a burning desire and deep faith.

Where you are is the result of the changes you have made in your life. Where you are going is dependent on the changes you are willing to make.

If you want to know where you will end up on this trip, you have to look at where you have been. In order for us to appreciate what tomorrow will bring, we have to understand what yesterday left behind. This calls for Ideal–Solution Formatting. It is a process of finding a method that helps define a problem, speculate solutions, and identify the obstacles that keep you from achieving your goal.

Understanding what yesterday left behind calls for you and me to cash in the kindness and forgiveness that today allowed us to experience. Today is about correcting the errors of yesterday and entering tomorrow with wisdom. This requires a change. *Where you are is the result of the changes you have made in your life. Where you are going is dependent on the changes you are willing to make.*

Change transforms possibilities and potential into progress. We close the door to improvement in our lives when we close our hearts to being adjusted. We must open our hearts to undergo an alteration from the inside-out. A change is a call for action. We must minimize the effects of our error and put ourselves on the right track for tomorrow. Your life becomes better when you become better. Only you know what action you need to take. But I can tell you this: A change in your mind or even in your heart is irrelevant without action. An effective life is a learning process. Change is the key to continuing your education.

—— CORRECTING THE MIND ——

How long did it take you to get here?

Why did you leave?

Which way did you go when you left?

What were you trying to get away from?

Why do you think the place you left behind is a worse location than where you are?

What brought you here?

Discuss today's topic with other readers at

www.solitary-refinement.com.

A challenge from the Author:
Follow through with your breakthrough.

Create in me a clean heart, O God, And renew a steadfast
spirit within me. ~ Psalm 51:10 (NASB)

 Remember …
Read, meditate, and process just one day at a time.
Don't rush your journey.

DAY 11: Changing Your Direction

When I went away to college, I had the mindset that I needed to make up for something. I believed that my disability confined me from living a normal teenage life. Therefore, I spent the next two years partying like never before. I never understood what it meant to be the life of the party until then. You name it, I did it. Everything except drugs. Even though I was in a wheelchair, I would go out and hit the dance floor as if I were the best dancer in the world. Everybody loved to see me out there on the dance floor, including the ladies. Now, did I go home dying inside, because I knew there was a greater purpose in my life, and I thought I was throwing away that purpose? Absolutely not! I enjoyed every bit of it; up until the day I looked at the direction I was headed.

To successfully end this time of correcting the mind, we must deal with what is called Simple-Mental-Conflict. This is a conflict that occurs when the mind knows what the heart and soul can achieve, but puts up mental roadblocks to prevent you from going in that direction.

I'm sure after the last ten days, especially day nine,

you see one or two changes you need to make with the direction of your life. The subjects we have discussed were intended to start some momentum in your life. You don't need to be apprehensive at this stage. I am not trying to make you change your mind; just correct your thinking. Do not be afraid of letting the perspective of this book help you have the right perspective on life. An accurate mental approach to life is going to make all the difference in the world. Of course, a brand new outlook will allow you to see the path of your life through an atypical lens. Change will be unavoidable. Now, you must know, it is more draining to think about it than it is to do it. This is true with everything that is difficult in life. Do not let your mind tell you any different.

THE SHIFT

Applying a fresh point of view calls for a shift to take place in your life. Not just a shift in gears, but also a shift in thought, a shift in direction, and a shift in perception. Such shifts will adjust your life according to your growth. Often-times, people say to themselves, "I don't know where my life will end up." Well, your life will always end up in the direction you are going. If you look ahead and don't like what you see, then it's time to make a shift. It's time to change the direction of your life.

Why is this such a fearful thing to do? It is simple; we aren't prepared for a different climate. The idea of going to Iceland when in our minds we were headed to Tahiti, throws us for a loop. Never mind that we would rather be in the colder climate. The bottom line is, we would rather go in the same direction than lose our sense of direction. We think it is okay to be wrong as long as we feel right. We must understand that what we are feeling is actually familiarity. We have returned to the same path that got us here from the very beginning just because it feels right.

Making a shift doesn't mean we abandon who we are. It also doesn't mean that our past becomes vain. It means that we allow who we have become, good and bad, to be a compass for our lives. What good is a compass if we continue to go in the same direction? In other words, what good are all of the experiences we have gone through if we don't feel free enough to venture out? The compass of who you are will challenge you to go into uncharted areas of your life. Uncharted areas in your life are true signs of an unfulfilled life. These areas are places you could have gone but weren't adventurous enough to go there.

As I have said before, my greatest fear is to look back

on my life at 80 years of age and see all the places I could have gone, but used my wheelchair as a reason not to go there. The shift in my life meant that I have to be willing at the age of 34 to leave my wheelchair at the bottom of a mountain and climb on someone's back so I can get to the top and see the beautiful view. *People who see mountains as obstacles are those who are not willing to make the necessary changes to get to the top.*

I will always be able to go back to my chair, but I may never have a chance to see that view again. Is it embarrassing to have to climb on someone else's back at 34 years of age? No. The embarrassing part would be the knowledge that I could have gone to the mountaintop, but I let pride stop me from changing my direction. The funny thing about this is that the same people who would not do what it takes to get to the mountaintop, view me as mentally and physically disabled. I say, "I am the one that chose to see life from a perspective that is higher ...

People who see mountains as obstacles are those who are not willing to make the necessary changes to get to the top.

and broader than my situation. Who is the disabled one?"

CHANGING DIRECTIONS VS. ROCKING THE BOAT

One Sunday afternoon, my Mom and I were out on a boat with some friends of mine. The owner of the boat asked me if I wanted to be the captain of the ship. A ship it was. It was quite a big boat. So I said to myself, "Why not? Most people don't trust me with a $10,000 car, but you are going to trust me with a $250,000 house boat. Man, there is something wrong with you!" But anyway, I took him up on the offer. After going straight for a while, my friend told me to take a different direction. So, he asked me to start turning the wheel to my right. I started to turn and turn and turn and turn and kept turning. But from my point of view, it seemed like the boat wasn't changing directions. It felt as if we were still heading in the same direction.

Finally, my friend said, "Ok, that's good. Start turning back." I was wondering, why would we turn back when we never even really started to go in the new direction that he wanted us to take? He saw my confused look and said, "I want you to turn around and look behind you." When I turned to look behind me, it seemed like everything was repositioning itself to support my new direction.

When a change in one component affects all other components in the same system, this is what is called inter-dependence. Life is the same way. When we make a major change in direction for our life, we must realize that sooner or later everything behind us will line up. Everything in the past will support the new direction toward which we are headed.

Because of my disability, cerebral palsy, it would have been a lot easier for me to keep the boat straight, rather than fighting my arms to turn it around. I think it's the same for many people. Many times we don't want to put the work into changing the direction of our lives. We would rather run into a brick wall than attempt to make the change. There is no doubt about it: Refusal to change direction will lead to a dead-end. Many times we are too stubborn to look ahead and see what is coming. If the forehead of your life is full of bumps and scrapes, it's a good sign that you need to change your direction. A person who changes their direction, changes their life.

Sometimes we say, "Well, I don't want to rock the boat." Changing directions doesn't mean you'll rock the boat. Rocking the boat is when you go from one direction to another direction, and back to the same direction. Changing direction means going on a newly-revealed visible course for your life. Though it may not be clear, you can see how this path will be a lot less bumpy than the path you are on now. There will always be new heights, deeper dimensions, and wider paths in life. People don't want to change direction because they were prepared to only go a certain distance. This new direction in their lives requires them to go a lot further than they were initially willing to go. When you put a limit on how far you are willing to go, it is the same thing as someone else putting a limit on how far you can go.

—— CORRECTING THE MIND ——

What do you see ahead of you?

Are you satisfied with what you see?

What are the pros and cons of going that way?

What is the alternative direction?

Discuss today's topic with other readers at
www.solitary-refinement.com.

A challenge from the Author:
The Creator of the World has mapped
out a plan for your life.

The mind of man plans his way,
But the LORD directs his steps.
~ Proverbs 16:9 (NASB)

 Remember ...

Read, meditate, and process just one day at a time.

Don't rush your journey.

Confronting the HEART

DAY 12: Facing Your Heart

Let me just come out and tell you what I have to tell so many people. God did not change my situation; He changed my heart. You see, the truth of it is, up until the age of 18, I had a lot of bitterness, resentment, confusion, pain, and disappointment bottled up inside. I did not understand why I was dealt the cards that I had been dealt. My heart ached from my situation. In order for me to become liberated emotionally and spiritually, while remaining physically imprisoned, I had to face what I felt about myself in my heart.

The heart is the center of man. It sits between the physical and the emotional aspects of who he is. This is why we must daily persuade our heart to understand life as is. Just like the mind, the heart must also be educated. One of the most important things for the heart to know is that there is a place inside everyone known as a cache. This is our hiding place. Many of us live in this dark corner of our heart and don't even know it.

We live in a locked box with our deepest hurts, biggest dreams, darkest secrets, weakest failures, and greatest victories, as well as defeats. We cannot be afraid to unlock the box, look into it, and take out the worthless pieces.

We have to come to a point where we bring to the surface the issues of our past, our hurts, and our deepest, darkest secrets. A troubled heart is a wounded heart which has been closed up without first being opened up and cleaned out. The infection of the past is still causing a great deal of discomfort. A clean heart is determined by our desires. Sometimes in order for the heart to experience healing, we have to let go of some of those desires.

Of all the things we will deal with in this book, I think this is the most important. It is tough to face the darkness and hardness of our own heart. Yes, we all have the propensity to do wrong, but that's not what I'm talking about. We all have things that are bottled up inside of us waiting to be unleashed on some other person or thing. We have to ask ourselves, "Where did this come from?"

ARE YOU YOUR OWN PALLBEARER?

Have you ever heard of a palled-life? This is a life that is sheltered from light. Darkness of the heart is the result of layers of hard living. Every difficult issue we face in our life covers our heart with a dark fabric. Some of the fabrics are lighter or thicker than others, but all contribute to the darkness. The more fabric that is laid over the heart, the harder the surface becomes and the voice of the heart is muffled. You have become your own pallbearer, carrying your heart in a locked box.

What if I tell you that the heart that you have locked in that box is still beating? You are about to bury yourself alive. *You think you are just hiding the pain, but what you are really doing is suffocating yourself.* You are depriving yourself of oxygen. The lack of oxygen is causing your heart to decay and harden.

In order to get rid of the darkness and hardness of the heart, begin to peel back each layer of a hard life. It is vital to remember that the closer you get to your heart, the more painful it will be. Somehow the first layer, the layer that is closest to your heart, becomes a part of your heart. It is kind of like peeling an orange and finding that final white surface around the orange. It is so close to the meat of the orange that it starts to rip away some of the meat. It is worth losing a little part of

You think you are just hiding the pain, but what you are really doing is suffocating yourself.

yourself rather then never revealing the heart of who you are.

Most people are not aware that their heart longs for a purpose. When it is on a scavenger hunt for purpose, reality can escape us. This process stirs up nonfactual thoughts and emotions that deceive us. Even though the truth is written on the heart of every man, his heart is naturally rebellious against anything that defines or limits him. This causes us to act, think, and feel contradictory to who we really are. It is at this point we are known to reject truth, and the rebellious spirit in us rises to the surface.

We have to be careful not to develop an opaque heart. The heart can grow to be impenetrable to light and will not allow it to pass through. This is the point where the heart becomes dark, hard, and stops responding to truth. When this is the case, we have to ask ourselves, "What am I really after? Is it good for me? Why do I want it? Can it truly be obtained?" The voice of the heart must emerge, somewhere, sometime, for all of us. Listen for it, and your breakthrough will come.

—— CONFRONTING THE HEART ——

Make a list of the layers over your heart.

What does the voice of your heart sound like?

How have you rebelled and wandered away from who you really are?

What are you keeping locked in your heart that is of no value to you?

Discuss today's topic with other readers at
www.solitary-refinement.com.

A challenge from the Author:
The life or death of a person begins in the heart.

I call heaven and earth to witness against you today, that
I have set before you life and death, the blessing and the
curse. So choose life in order that you may live, you and
your descendants...~ Deuteronomy 30:19 (NASB)

 Remember ...
Read, meditate, and process just one day at a time.
Don't rush your journey.

DAY 13: Unavoidable Truth

For the first few months of college, I almost starved myself to death. My friends and I would go to the cafeteria or to the local restaurant and I would intentionally order finger food that I could eat quickly. That was it. No water, no drink, nothing. Just real simple, easy finger foods. I did not want them to know how messy food could get for me. You don't understand; you could be eating at a table across from me and end up with my food in your lap. That is just how out-of-control it can be sometimes. I cannot tell you how much good food I passed up. I wasn't trying to deny my disability; I was trying to avoid the outcome of it. Now, today I would do whatever it takes to get that food to my mouth - even if it means that one of my best friends has to sit in a public restaurant and feed me a messy BBQ sandwich. You know something? When my friend was feeding me that sandwich, he dropped the food on my

The truth you will not open your heart to is 90% of the acceptance and validation you are looking for someone else to give you.

lap. All this time I was avoiding not making a mess, just for someone else to make a mess on me. What's the point? I might as well enjoy the sandwich. We deny ourselves so much good nourishment by avoiding the truth in our hearts.

So many people live what I call a "Plausible Life." This is a life that appears to be of truth, but is really deceptive. Truth begins with self-concept, the characteristics and attributes an individual believes they possess. *The truth you will not open your heart to is 90% of the acceptance and validation you are looking for someone else to give you.*

This is going to hit close to home for some. When you do not hold the truth in your heart, your mind will convince you that you need someone else to put a stamp of approval on you. If your heart doesn't approve of your life, then all you are is a guinea pig for the rest of the world. No one should aspire to be just another experiment in life's laboratory. But so many of us settle for trying one method after another method, rather than going with something that has been tested and proven. All you are really doing is avoiding the facts. I have to say, this is why people are running from one religion to another religion; from one cult to another cult. They are guinea pigs in this life. Given enough time, you will begin to not only know what I am saying, but feel it, as well.

When you feel truth, it is unavoidable. *Knowing* the truth in our minds is not the same as *having* truth in our hearts. Truth in the mind is comprised of facts. Truth in the heart is a lifestyle. It is a choice to live in freedom and pay the high cost of living there. Living in a trustworthy realm of life is the purpose of truth. However, the purpose of truth is not fulfilled until it has been spoken, heard, acknowledged, and acted on. Most of us are not prepared to pay-in-full the cost of that purpose. We can speak the truth and even hear it. But, we struggle with acknowledging and acting on the truth. This is not just a fact for our minds to ponder; it is a real issue that must be dealt with in our hearts.

You cannot act on truth until it is acknowledged. So, how do you recognize truth? Truth is not what we believe, hear from others, or tell ourselves. It is the collective census of our minds, hearts and souls. In order to gather this census, you have to take into account what your heart feels, your mind thinks, and your soul believes to be true. Once we gather all of that insight and information, we have to return to a truth filter. Remember on Day Two when we talked about a truth filter and the dark boxes in which we carry our hearts? Well, a truth filter is a strainer on our hearts, minds, and souls that separates facts from opinions. It allows us to operate in light rather than in darkness. The heart cannot recognize anything when it is in darkness. This is the problem with acknowledging truth.

INTERNAL TRUTH VS. EXTERNAL LIES

Truth in the dark is the same as a lie in the light. The difference between the two is that one is internal and one is external. Internal truth, that is truth held in the darkness of the heart, never comes out through your actions, words, and thoughts, whereas external lies always find their way into your actions, words, and thoughts and slowly seep into your heart. Sadly enough, truth in the heart is never sought out until a lie creeps in. It is not until a lie reduces us into a state of submission that we turn on the light and look for evidence. It's a sad day in one's life when a lie is needed to generate the truth.

Acting on truth requires us to take responsibility for what we know to be right. People really think refusing to comply with a true statement somehow makes it false. Do I have news for them! Whether accepted or not, truth is always truth. Denial does not make facts irrelevant. Acting on truth means answering the question, "Who are you, truly?" This is a heart, mind, and soul question. It requires three different answers put through the truth filter. It is very important for us to know that separately, our heart, mind, and soul can lead us in the wrong direction. It is the common denominator of all three that gives us the true path we must take.

It is time to launch yourself out of your present condition into your true potential. Legitimacy can be the rocket to make that happen. Truth ignited in your heart lifts you to the next level in life. We sometimes pretend to be acrophobic in order avoid to it. Actually, we are not afraid of heights; we are afraid of our reality. You and I are afraid of having truth in our hearts because once it gets there, it is unavoidable.

—— CONFRONTING THE HEART ——

What will you see if you turn on the light in your heart?

What elephant in the room are you pretending not to see?

How are you avoiding truth in your life?

Discuss today's topic with other readers at
www.solitary-refinement.com.
A challenge from the Author:

Every person is blind until the eyes of their heart are opened.

I pray that the eyes of your heart may be enlightened, so that you will know what is the hope of His calling, what are the riches of the glory of His inheritance in the saints...
~ Ephesians 1:18 (NASB)

 Remember ...

Read, meditate, and process just one day at a time.

Don't rush your journey.

DAY 14: The Lie You Told Yourself

Shortly after college, I told myself that the hard work was over. I no longer had to give my all to whatever I was doing. "Everyone will see my disability, and therefore, my life will be a piece of cake. Hey, I'm in a wheelchair; I shouldn't have to fight to get ahead of the crowd. I shouldn't have to stand in line." I can tell you now that I was lying to myself. I was giving myself an excuse to become lazy. I just wanted to be comfortable with who I was.

Don't shut down now. You had to know this day was coming. It is time to let go of the security blanket you are holding onto, hoping to survive. Animals survive; people conquer. It's time for you to face the lies in order to understand the reality of your life. To continue telling yourself what you need to hear to be comfortable with yourself will only enable you to exist, to live one more day. Opening your heart to see self deception is the key to living a triumphant life.

Yes, the inability to be transparent with another person is not good for your relationships. But more important than that, it is destructive not to be real with yourself.

Lying to yourself eventually eats away at you, your family, and your friends. You may hide it very well, but it will destroy you internally. Facing destructive lies will result in prevailing truth. The facts will anchor us in this unstable world in which we live.

Authenticity is medicine for the decaying soul. However, just like any other infection, the longer we wait to get the medication, the less likely we will survive. We cannot delay getting to the truth any longer. If your soul does not resonate with this, I strongly suggest that you read back through the last 13 days. The rest of this book will do you no good if you don't embrace what is certain and disarm the power of a lie. Who cares if it takes you 62 days to get through this book? This is about your life! Go back over everything we talked about thus far.

BE REAL

Now, you say that I'm taking away from your ability to cope. This time in your life with your face in this book is not about tolerating the issues - it's about dealing with them. *Let's be real. In order to just cope with a situation, there must be some amount of deceit.* We have a need to protect ourselves from our deepest fears. However, our attempt

Let's be real. In order to just cope with a situation, there must be some amount of deceit.

to do so, in most cases, results in a shadowy self-perjure that only hides that fear. Oddly enough, this is okay with us simply because we do not want to be in touch with our reality. You cannot be real with yourself and just cope with the issues. You have to put yourself face-to-face with the heart of who you are.

It takes a lot of work to dig down in our hearts. It pulls us out of our comfort zone and makes us face reality head-on. We tell ourselves, "I am okay with it. It is going to be alright. It will change in time." That justification makes us temporarily comfortable with who we are. And you may say, "What's wrong with just being comfortable, with just tolerating the issues?"

Let me ask you this: How often does your mind change? How many times does your attitude go back and forth? How many different moods do people see you in during the course of a day's time? Why are you changing your position so much? Are you not comfortable with who you are? Many times, I fall asleep on my couch. At that point in time, I am comfortable, no doubt about it. But after I lie there for a while, I begin to toss and turn. My sleep is disrupted and I am no longer comfortable in that position.

Many of us are trying to live life in disrupted peace, most commonly known as self-deception. We can only tolerate where we are for so long and then a change must take place - a change in our attitude, our moods, and our thoughts. Then, once we get comfortable again, the whole cycle starts over. But what would happen if we stopped trying to be comfortable and tolerate the issues, and just went on and finally dealt with them? The only way for me to get proper rest is to get myself off the sofa and onto the mattress, the place that was designed for proper sleep. We have to get ourselves out of a comfortable place and into reality; into the realm of truth where real peace dwells.

—— CONFRONTING THE HEART ——

What is the lie you told yourself in order to make it to today?

Why did you tell yourself that lie?

Are you truly at peace with it?

Discuss today's topic with other readers at
www.solitary-refinement.com.

A challenge from the Author:
Your heart can hold in it unexplainable peace.

Peace I leave with you; My peace I give to you; not as the world gives do I give to you. Do not let your heart be troubled, nor let it be fearful. ~ John 14:27 (NASB)

 Remember …
Read, meditate, and process just one day at a time.
Don't rush your journey.

DAY 15: Receiving Your Healing

Around the age of 27, I had a really bad fall that resulted in multiple seizures and short-term memory loss. When I arrived at the emergency room, my father, with whom I had little to no communication my whole life, arrived in Atlanta. My mom, back in Baton Rouge, called him to ask if he could just go check on me until she got there. He arrived sometime that day, after they put me in a private room and drugged me up very well. Like I said, I had lost my short-term memory, but for some reason, when he entered my room, I must have remembered the pain that he had caused me. I cannot tell you exactly what I said, but my coworker who was with me said I laid into him so heavily that he started to cry. My coworker also said I told my father, "This friend, who has only known me for two years has more love for me than my own father." This pain that I had held in my heart for 27 years had to be released.

You are right. You didn't deserve it. It wasn't your fault. They were wrong. It was an unfair situation. No questioning it, there are many malignant people in this world. We can't change it. People inflict people with deliberate harm.

The result of this has caused you pain - pain that must be addressed and dealt with. You must do something with your grievous spirit. You cannot deny the heaviness of your heart any longer.

How long will you allow hurt to fester inside of you? This hurt is eating its way through your heart to the core of your life. Understand something here; I am not talking about forgiveness. I'm talking about no longer reacting to the issue. You must understand that pain causes reaction. Your response to your life is more than likely your reaction to the pain you are feeling. Responding to your life out of the pain someone else has caused is hurting you more than you know. What I am trying to get you to see here is that responding to someone out of pain they did not inflict on you, causes them to view you as bitter, mean, and crazy. And, with good reason. The way they relate to you does not warrant your action toward them. You must heal from your past relationships for your future relationships to be healthy.

The word "latent" means present but not visible. Is this not the perfect word to describe our pain? It may not be visible, but it is undeniably there. You have to acknowledge that it is an issue. There is a condition called Sensorimotor Neuropathy. This happens when a person who is diabetic fails to give themselves the proper attention. They no longer feel the sensation of temperature, light touch, pin prick, and pain. In essence, the patient becomes so numb throughout various parts of their body that their arm could be on fire and they would not feel it.

Hurt is the outcome of two things: A wound that needs to be closed, or a pressure point that needs some release. We must be able to sense the damage that this pain is causing. We need to be aware of and treat the pressure points and open wounds of our lives. We have to be careful not to become Mentally and/or Emotionally Neuropathic by numbing ourselves from the pain of the situation.

It is more damaging to be numb to the pain than it is to feel the pain.

IGNORANCE IS NOT BLISS

You must attend to the emotional wounds and pressure points of your life. For some reason, people would rather ignore them. They do not want to feel the hurt. However, *it is more damaging to be numb to the pain than it is to feel the pain.* We must understand two things: One, just because you are numb to hurt doesn't mean that the pain is not there. Two, it is better to feel the hurt and be aware of the situation rather than pretend it's not there, causing ourselves more pain. You see, an open wound will eventually become infected. Ignore a pressure point and it will surely lead to a heart attack, stroke, or brain aneurism.

Many people have died as a result of ignoring the pain they were feeling. With this in mind, let me lay something out on the table for you. You may say that the pain that someone has brought to your life is killing you. The truth is, it is only hurting you. If this pain results in death, it is because you have chosen to ignore it and therefore commit internal suicide.

—— CONFRONTING THE HEART ——

What damage are you doing to yourself emotionally by not recognizing your hurts?

What are the pressure points and open wounds in your life?

Who do you need to confront about the pain they caused you?

Please know that they may not respond the way you want them to respond. But this is not about them; this is about you.

In what ways have you hurt yourself?

Discuss today's topic with other readers at
www.solitary-refinement.com.

A challenge from the Author:
Your pain can be in God's hand.

...and He will wipe away every tear from their eyes; and
there will no longer be any death; there will no longer
be any mourning, or crying, or pain; the first things have
passed away. ~ Revelation 21:4 (NASB)

 Remember ...
Read, meditate, and process just one day at a time.
Don't rush your journey.

DAY 16: The Pain You Have Caused

Remember the story I shared yesterday about the pain I had to release because of the lack of relationship I had with my father? Something interesting happened during that time. As far as I know, he never retaliated for what I said to him. His reply, or lack of reply, played a very crucial role in my life since then, as well as his. My healing came when he gave me the medicine of acceptance. Maybe what I wanted all those years was for him to accept the pain that he caused me. That made all the difference in the world. No, we don't have the best relationship, but I can respect him for allowing me to express the pain that he caused me, rather than denying it.

Many times in our lives, we have an argument with someone and wonder – weeks, months, or even years later – why they reacted that way. How many times have you asked yourself, "Why is this same issue coming up over and over again?" It is because of something that was never said that needs to be said: "Your words and actions caused me pain."

Your initial reaction to this may be, "I couldn't care

less." Oh really? Let's talk about the word compunction. It is an anxiety of the conscience caused by regret for causing pain. By puncturing someone's heart, you have opened your heart for remorse. Your words and actions can cut like a stiletto. This short dagger does not cut deep, but it cuts wide. Your stab at that person did more damage then you thought it would. You cut yourself in the process, didn't you? Now both of you are injured.

The truth is, the words, "I couldn't care less," are your attempt to stop your heart from feeling the pain of causing someone else pain. In your heart, it hurts you to know you may have hurt someone else. It hurts you to know that your actions and words were a knife in the heart of someone you care about and love. And it should. You are liable for the feelings of hurt and shame that person is feeling.

Why do we think people are invulnerable? We all feel pain. Oh, I get it. You are one of those who have become numb to most of your pain and so good at hiding the rest of it that you expect others to do the same. I have one of you in my life, too. Here is the sadistic problem with that. You know what a malicious heart feels like. You have conscious-ly become a menace to another person. If you know what it feels like to have to bottle up your pain, why would you want to put someone else in that same predicament? Your refusal to acknowledge what you have done only aggravates the wounds. Every time you refuse to say, "I did that. And I'm sorry," the cut is split open all over again. Your irresponsible actions have turned into sadistic torture for the other person, and for you as well.

WRITING THE PRESCRIPTION

It is time to take responsibility. No, you cannot change what you have done, but you can be a part of the healing process. You may say, "If I do that, this person will hold it over my head for the rest of my life." That may be the case. Maybe it needs to be held over your head for a while. The fact of the matter is, you don't know how that person will eventually respond once they are healed. Holding it over your head could be a part of the healing process for them. Whatever the case may be, it is crucial for you to give them a chance to be healed.

What we must understand is that the wounded person will eventually deal with the pain you caused them. They will get to a point where they have to release the things that hurt them. The release that person will eventually experience might not necessarily come out on you. Let me ask you something: How many times do we wonder why a person acts the way they act once they've grown up? We wonder why they've ended up on drugs or doing things contradictory to the way they were raised. Oftentimes, we see them on talk shows like Montel Williams, Dr. Phil or even Oprah because they need to release the pain that was caused by the actions and words of others. We need to understand that people who abuse themselves do so because they were abused by someone else. Abuse is not just physical or sexual; abuse can be mental and verbal.

Only pride will stop you from letting the other person receive the healing they need.

We often think that just because we are going through something, we have the license to act, think, and say whatever we feel – but we don't give the other person the license to respond to it. All pain causes reaction. *Only pride will stop you from letting the other person receive the healing they need.* Whoever holds within themselves the power to allow someone else to experience healing and chooses not to use that power, is a prideful and sadistic person. We need to become rueful at some point and express sorrow.

—— CONFRONTING THE HEART ——

Who have you hurt?

What does that person need to hear from you to begin to heal?

What do you need to do to humble yourself so that you can release this type of healing to another?

Discuss today's topic with other readers at
www.solitary-refinement.com.

A challenge from the Author:
Do not take the wickedness in your heart lightly.

Tremble, and do not sin;
Meditate in your heart upon your bed, and be still.
Selah. Offer the sacrifices of righteousness,
And trust in the LORD. ~ Psalm 4:4-5 (NASB)

STOP Remember …

Read, meditate, and process just one day at a time.

Don't rush your journey.

DAY 17: Letting Go to Hold On

Several years ago, I met a girl that I quickly fell for. She was what I considered the perfect girl for me; very intelligent, ambitious, and with a very mild form of cerebral palsy, which meant that she could kind of relate to what I was going through. Everyone thought that we were the cutest couple, ever. To be honest, I thought the same, except when it came to our spiritual levels. The more we talked about things that matter, the more obvious it became to me that we were on different pages, spiritually. Now, I am going to let you in on a little secret. I am so realistic with myself that I know the chances of a female really accepting and getting to know who I really am are slimmer for me than most guys. So, holding onto this relationship seemed to be what I needed to do even though I saw some red flags in our future. At the same time, I saw the spiritual level that my heart longed to reach, as well as a calling and purpose for my life. Although I enjoyed this relationship, I had to ask myself if this relationship or this calling in my life would eventually fail me. Several years later, I am still single, but I can tell you that the calling on my life has not failed me yet. Nor, do I think it ever will.

People have an unyielding grip on broken relationships, failed dreams, false hopes, unfixable mistakes, an unerasable past, passed up opportunities, and empty promises, all because we do not accept the reality of the adjectives that describe what we have in our hands. Broken, failed, false, unfixable, unerasable, passed up, and empty all describe something that will not withstand the test of time; there is no future in these adjectives. We say we are at the end of our ropes. If this is the case, then why would you be at the end of one rope and not reach out for another?

We are people who will hang onto a rope that is ripping before our very eyes. Meanwhile, there's a perfectly strong rope within our reach, but fear and familiarity prevent us from letting go and reaching out. Why? One reason would be pride. The faulty rope has borne our weight for this long; therefore, we don't think it's going to break on us now. However, because of the rip, there is a high probability of it falling apart. This probability gets higher in proportion to the length of time it bears the weight.

I have some news for you: Everything that we constantly apply pressure to will eventually break. This rope will not hold you up forever. You must let go. You cannot let the shock of a rip keep you from understanding that you are going to fall. The rope will completely unravel over time. You need to let go of shame and hold onto a new start.

The problem here is the fear of giving up control for the short timeframe while reaching from one rope to another. Fear of letting go has blinded you from seeing the lifeline that is in your face. In this case, you are the stronghold in your life. A certain degree of security is found in holding on to something. But if that something is truly worth our faith and trust, we will not need to hold on to it – it will hold on to us.

RELEASE YOUR EMOTIONAL GRIP

Trying to keep an emotional grip on our fantasy is causing us to lose touch with our reality. Having such a tight grip on the things we think we need and want is choking out any room for improvement and contentment in our lives. Maybe this belief is enabling us to survive, but it has stopped us from living. Here's a thought: The pain and agony in your life is actually a cramp from hanging on so tightly. Your pain will not subside until you let go. The moment between letting go of one rope and grabbing the other is the release you need. Releasing something in your mind will liberate your heart and cause your soul to anchor down into something more concrete. Slavery has not ended until we liberate ourselves.

You have chosen to remain attached to a lifeline that has proven faulty. You are hanging on for dear life to a torn rope. There is more danger in hanging on to a weak rope than there is in reaching out for a stronger one. Trust in the facts, not the circumstances. In other words, *be careful not to give a rope the same power as a chain.* There are situations you are hanging onto as if you are locked to them. In return, you are looking for a way to pry your way out rather than just cutting yourself loose.

It is time to ask yourself questions of value; questions that ask the worth or desirability of something. Is your unwillingness to let go also your attempt to commit mental suicide? Do you want the rope to break, because if it does, you won't have any accountability for tomorrow? Have you given up on yourself and chosen not to do what it takes to see another day?

Be careful not to give a rope the same power as a chain.

Can I give you something to think about right here? If you fall while teeter-tottering between these two ropes, you have no one to blame but your-self. Let me repeat that. If you fall while teeter-tottering between these two ropes, you have no one to blame but yourself. Reach out, let go, and grab hold. Don't wait until it is too late.

—— CONFRONTING THE HEART ——

What is the weak rope in your life that you are hanging onto?

Where do you see your life going if you let go?

Why would you not let go?

Discuss today's topic with other readers at
www.solitary-refinement.com.

A challenge from the Author:
If you let go, you just might find something
worth hanging onto.

For whoever wishes to save his life will lose it,
but whoever loses his life for My sake,
he is the one who will save it. ~ Luke 9:24 (NASB)

Remember ...

Read, meditate, and process just one day at a time.

Don't rush your journey.

DAY 18: The Traps Behind Circumstances

Until the age of 16, I wore leg braces like Tom Hanks in the movie Forrest Gump. It took my family an hour every day to put them on me. It took me about five minutes to take them off. I hated those things. They constantly pinched, scraped, and bruised my body from my hips all the way down to my ankles. But, I believed wearing these braces would one day help me to be able to walk. At the age of 16, just believing wasn't enough. So, one day, in physical therapy, I asked my doctor if I would ever be able to walk. He answered no. My response was, "Then, why am I wearing these braces?" If I was never going to walk, then what was the point? All these braces did for me at that time was to make me stand out even more. It just brought more attention to my already obviously crippled body. From that day forward, I never wore braces again. Some of us are trapped by embracing the situation rather than by the situation itself. It is time to stop calling attention to yourself.

What is it that makes you say, "This is not for me. That's just the way it goes. There's nothing I could do. It was meant to be this way." A lucky few are born into situations in which positive messages abound. Many of us grow up hearing indirect messages that invoke fear and failure in our hearts. These subliminal messages are traps used to catch and hold us. The moment we accept that people are the product of their environment, the trap is engaged.

How do we know we are trapped? If the mention of a situation causes your heart to tighten, then you are trapped. What makes these traps effective in holding you back is what is inside of you. Our self-esteem allows the hook to sink in. For example, some of us have come to believe that we cannot get ahead in life because of the color of our skin. Or because you are in a wheelchair, you believe you can only do this or only do that. We accept these things that people and society say about us just because we are different. Over time, after hearing these things repeatedly, we begin to brutally and unfairly punish ourselves.

This message doesn't always have to be verbal. It could be the message you got from the way someone has treated you. This is a nonverbal trap, the trickiest of all because you can't recognize it so easily. Sometimes you don't even know how much you have been affected or held back from really going out there and being who you know you can be. You must search out these nonverbal traps. You must ask yourself, "Why do I feel this way?"

It is also important to understand the source of the message. Not everyone that tells you these things are jealous or are trying to hold you back from succeeding. Some people think everyone else is also confined to their same circumstances. They are speaking from their own experiences. They have tried to walk the walk or take the leap of faith that you are trying to take and it has ended up being the wrong step or the wrong timing for them. For some reason, they think that if they don't succeed at something, then surely someone else won't succeed at it either. What you have to recognize is that these people, the ones that send us the subliminal messages, don't know that it may be your time. You may be the person to do this. Or it may be the right time for you to get it done.

Like many, you took part in something called fact-interference confusion. It is when a person mistakes a conclusion they have drawn from an observation. People do not always know things are the way they are. So they tell us what they observe and we accept it as fact. When you understand that their circumstances are not your circumstances, the trap is disengaged. Now, you may want to go back and tell them what you have learned. Warning: Revenge, rubbing it in, and saying, "I told you so," resets the traps. Get out of it while you can.

CAPTOR OR LIBERATOR?

In the first few days of our journey, we talked about truth. Did you know that some of the messages that trap us can actually be the truth? Such truth is intended to liberate a person. *Your perception decides if truth is going to be your captor or your liberator.* The truth is I am disabled. Yes, I am black. The truth is some of you may have a challenge educationally. But the trap is believing that you are confined to it; believing that you cannot alter the facts to work in your favor.

Part of my disability is that my voice is very difficult to understand. You must pay close attention in order to really know what I am trying to say. Are you ready for this? As a professional keynote speaker, my voice is what makes me so effective. The fact that you have to pay close attention to me makes me an even more gifted communicator. I have taken the fact and altered it to play in my favor. Accepting the facts and believing in your ability to change the outcome are two different things.

Your perception decides if truth is going to be your captor or your liberator.

We have to come to the point

in our lives where we live life under no circumstances. Now you say, "That's ridiculous. You will always have circumstances. Things will always happen. Things will always come up. How can I live my life under no circumstances?" Now let me tell you, you just stuck your foot right in the middle of the trap I'm talking about. You see, I didn't say, "Live your life without circumstances." I said, "Live it under no circumstances." I'm saying, "Whatever the circumstance in your life, don't let it suppress you. Don't let it keep you down and confined to it."

I spent the first half of my life dealing with my dis-ability – trying to make myself better, trying to improve who I was. It came to a point where my improvement had reached its limit. I recognized that my disability would not get any better. So for the other half of my life — and probably for the rest of my life — I am finding ways of doing things that my disability will not allow me to do.

Let me repeat that: "In this half of my life, I am finding ways of doing things that my disability will not allow me to do." Now when I say, "Live your life under no circumstances," I'm saying, "Find ways of doing things that you know you cannot do under your circumstances. Find that loophole. Find that way around the circumstances."

—— CONFRONTING THE HEART ——

What have you chosen to believe about yourself?

Whom are you believing?

Looking at the facts of who you are, what can be altered to play in your favor?

What traps are you stepping into?

Is there another way?

Discuss today's topic with other readers at
www.solitary-refinement.com.

A challenge from the Author:
You are meant to be free.

For you were called to freedom, brethren; only do not turn
your freedom into an opportunity for the flesh, but through
love serve one another. ~ Galatians 5:13 (NASB)

Remember …

Read, meditate, and process just one day at a time.

Don't rush your journey.

DAY 19: Limits Needed to Reach Potential

As a child, I had an unrealistic dream just like every other kid. My dream was to one day become a racecar driver. However, unlike most kids, I could not dream too long. It wasn't long before life with a disability made me realize this dream was not going to happen. Trust me when I say, "It would not be good to put me behind the wheel of a car." This shattered dream enabled me to do so much more with my life. It allowed me to live a circumscribed life. I started to color my life inside the lines of my disability. Now I can say to you, "You have not reached your maximum potential until you find your true limitations."

It is time to focus. Focus means to adjust to the degree in which you can clearly see a defined point. All limits are guidelines used to frame your life. Without the framework, seeing the big picture will overwhelm you and cause you to take on an image your life was not designed for. As a result, you are unable to concentrate and put all your efforts into being who you are designed to be.

As people, we are not abstract art; we are what is

called representation art. Our lives are supposed to represent who we are. We have to channel our hopes, dreams, and abilities into the framework of limitation. These boundaries drastically cut back on wasted time, unrealistic dreams, and senseless effort in our lives. This defined point is your potential in life. Many people try to focus by answering the question, "What needs to be done?" But the three key focal questions are:

What can you do?

What can't you do?

What are you willing to do?

Now, we have to be careful at this point, because so many times, *we trick our minds into thinking what we can do is equivalent to what we are willing to do*. The truth is, oftentimes, what we are willing to do is so much less than what we can actually do. And that is why we fail to reach our true potential. We prefer to tell ourselves that we've done all that we can do long before we've exhausted ourselves. We all have intellectual, physical, emotional, and

We trick our minds into thinking what we can do is equivalent to what we are willing to do.

spiritual piggy-banks that we refuse to tap into. We will empty them for someone other than ourselves. However, when it comes to investing in ourselves, we hold back.

WHAT'S THE POINT?

Most people forget they can focus on the same point from many different angles. And this is what we want to pursue today, the different angles of a specific point. You can focus on life from an intellectual, physical, emotional, or spiritual angle. You have not reached your limitations or your potential until you do all that you can do intellectually, physically, emotionally, and spiritually.

The secret to being all you can be is knowing what you can be. As people, we tend to view limitations as a terminal illness. I'm not trying to get you to terminate your life; I want to encourage you to determine your life. Too many people are killing themselves trying to do any and everything that comes to mind. You have to know how wide you can go because it will determine how high you can go. Limitations are your width and potential is your height. Denying your limits is the greatest barrier you will ever face.

—— CONFRONTING THE HEART ——

Intellectually:

      What can you do?

      What can't you do?

      What are you willing to do?

Physically:

      What can you do?

      What can't you do?

      What are you willing to do?

Emotionally:

      What can you do?

      What can't you do?

      What are you willing to do?

Spiritually:

      What can you do?

      What can't you do?

      What are you willing to do?

Whatever it is, do it to the point that you have to file bankruptcy.

Discuss today's topic with other readers at

www.solitary-refinement.com.

**A challenge from the Author:
God will do something great with what
you see as a limitation.**

*…but God has chosen the foolish things of the world to
shame the wise, and God has chosen the weak things of the
world to shame the things which are strong…
~ 1 Corinthians 1:27 (NASB)*

 Remember …

Read, meditate, and process just one day at a time.

Don't rush your journey.

DAY 20: Time to Move On

As a professional keynote speaker and a person with a positive outlook on life, many wonderful people have come into my path. Initially, it seems natural for us to further develop our relationships. But, over time, the newness of who I am and the busyness of life takes over. As a result, a lot of my friendships with other people start to diminish. I am a very relational guy – I love people and I love being around people. So, it bothers me when a friendship starts to diminish. I want to know why that person doesn't return my phone call. Did I do something or say something wrong? What I struggled with at that point was not necessarily ending a relationship, but beginning a new one. I didn't want to allow myself to draw close to another person and go through the same cycle. However, I can tell you that if I had not moved on I would have missed out on some wonderful, life long friendships. I have friends now that I may not talk to for several months, but who remain some of my closest friends.

It is time to stop trying to rewrite the past and start rough-drafting the future. Moving on is the key to accomplishing this assignment. Let's start by not getting confused with what it really means to move on. It is to take an action that forces us to arouse out of our emotional rut and seek progress in our lives. It means not to let your past go vain. It seems simple, but it is not. It is easy to have the wrong perspective on the subject. Many people think moving on means to simply change your position on a particular situation. However, to truly move on you have to relocate. It's not just about changing your thoughts; it's about separating yourself from the issue.

You must first ask yourself, "Am I ready to move on?" Your response to this question is very important. Think about it. I would like for you to have a confirming response within yourself. It is a communication response that allows a person to value themselves more. Now, you just might say, "Yes, I am ready." But the truth is, if you have not moved on, then maybe there are some principles and concepts that you have not fully understood yet. Or maybe, there are some problems in your life that you have not solved just yet. Or, just maybe, you still have to learn a few lessons through your current situations.

NO TURNING BACK

Moving on demands mental conditioning along with

concise planning. Not being prepared for this trip will cause a derailment or, even worse, a wreck in our lives. Then, we have to deal with the after-effects of the derailment or wreck, which causes us to rethink the road trip. So check your engine NOW, because once you are on this road, there is no turning back.

The reason you get so mad when someone presses your button is because you realize that it is a button you should have pressed yourself in order to release yourself from the situation.

There are three essential steps in the process of moving on: The first step is to detach yourself. Any involvement with the situation keeps you connected. You can be physically free and emotionally attached. For some reason, we struggle with the feeling of being disconnected. It is as if we think we are going to miss out on something, even though this situation has proven to be a lost cause. Or maybe we think by denying ourselves emotional release, there is some punishment or accountability on the other end. *The reason you get so mad when someone presses your button is because you realize that it is a button you should have pressed yourself in order to release yourself from the situation.*

The second step is to relocate yourself. We have all heard the phrase, "Don't go there." This phrase means that if you take a certain action or say what you are about to say, there will be repercussions you are not prepared to face. The relocation step of moving on is all about going there with yourself. It's going to the heart of the matter even if it's painful. The painful truth at the heart of the matter is that you should have never been here in the first place. You know the place you are in right now is not the place for someone like you. You even know where you belong. On your way to that place, you saw somebody over there attached to what you now see as a rut when you thought it was a shortcut.

Well, you were wrong. It's time to admit that the grass is not greener on this side. Yes, you were just color-blind. Now how long will you stand there chewing and regurgitating the same aged brown grass your stomach keeps rejecting? You old cow, when will you move to a new field? You need to stop settling for a place in life and locate the place for your life.

The third step is to establish some roots in your life now. This is not the time to second guess yourself. If you are in a better place now than you were before, then at least you know that you are on the right path to your true destination.

It's true that you may only be here for a season. Speaking of seasons, I strongly dislike the wintertime. However, I'm very thankful for this time of the year. That seems a bit contradictory, but what I have realized in my life is that an effective winter season gives me the privilege of watching something that was dead come back to life in the springtime.

The only trees that do not come back to life are those that have not established their roots. When you relocate in the wintertime, you will not see the beauty of what surrounds you until the springtime. How unfortunate it would be to discover that you relocated in the most beautiful place and time of your life, but you must wait another four seasons to fully enjoy it because you never established your roots.

Many people start to move on but never complete the process because of complacency. Just packing up and moving in does not mean you have relocated. Once we get to a new location, it is time to unpack. This is a step we delay. At this juncture we become tired, busy with other things, and unconcerned with finishing the process. We do just enough to say we moved on, but we never settle in. Unsettled emotions of the past will continue to remind you of the past. Those who cannot remember the past probably will not repeat it. Warning: Complacency allows the past to catch up to you.

—— CONFRONTING THE HEART ——

What do you need to leave behind?

Why is it so hard to unpack?

Is there anything you brought with you that you wish you had not?

Why do you refuse to press the button that will release you?

Discuss today's topic with other readers at
www.solitary-refinement.com.

A challenge from the Author:
God has moved on; why can't you?

Therefore if anyone is in Christ, he is a new creature; the old things passed away; behold, new things have come.
~ 2 Corinthians 5:17 (NASB)

Remember …

Read, meditate, and process just one day at a time.

Don't rush your journey.

Connecting
With the
SOUL

DAY 21: Facing Your Soul

Last night, I wrote until the midnight hours. This morning I woke up and I started writing right away. To be honest, I'm getting tired. I'm ready for this project to be over. I don't want to write right now, but there is so much going on in my head. There is so much going on inside me that I can't stop now. Even though I feel like it's time to just take a break from things mentally and emotionally, I push through it. I know in these moments, some of my best work is developed.

I know that you are at a point in this journal where you might be saying, "Alright, I'm done. I can't go any farther." You need to know that this is the time when the best in you is about to be revealed. This is the time when your best work comes through; when you are worn out, but still press through and face the challenges and changes of life.

Many people become hungry, thirsty, in despair, and disturbed because they refuse to acknowledge their soul. The worst type of rejection a person can ever face is when they reject themselves. The soul of a man defines him. It is the soul that gives value to education, vocational position, economic level, and relationships with others. Not recognizing and enhancing the soul depreciates everything you will ever accomplish. Like it or not, the significance of your life, as you know it, is losing its worth daily until you pay attention to the soul of who you are.

MICROPHONE OF YOUR SOUL

Your soul makes you unique. It not only separates man from animal, it separates man from man. Someone can think the way you think. Or even feel the way you feel. But no one can be who you are. You are not who your education and money say you are; you are who people see beneath it all. Your soul is that voice in the back of your head. The spirit is a microphone that allows that voice to be heard by the world. *The spirit of a person speaks louder than their own vocal cords.* Whether we know it or not, our soul is always in a Self-Disclosure Mode. It deliberately and continuously communicates information to others about who we really are. Even when you are trying to hide it, there is still a spirit within you that tells it all. The question is, "What is it saying?"

The spirit of a person speaks louder than their own vocal cords.

Have you ever found yourself in conflict with someone and you're not sure why? It is called Pseudo Conflict. It occurs when individuals disagree because of inaccurate communication. Your mouth may not say much. However, your spirit about the situation is saying a lot. Somebody's spouse is going to thank me for saying that. Nevertheless, here is why I brought up Pseudo Conflict. Deep down inside of you are the answers to the questions that have risen to the surface of your heart and mind. If the mind and the heart choose to disregard the soul, a great deal of damage is done. Trying to live life disconnected from your soul is not really living. When ignoring your soul or acting as if it is trivial, you cease to live life to its fullest. A muffled soul is a life without a voice.

Oftentimes, the mind and the heart are in disagreement. The soul will not contradict what is right, no matter what the heart feels and the mind thinks. It searches for the truth and settles the dispute between the heart and mind. It is the referee between the two. The only way to reconnect with the soul is to connect your mind and heart with the truth of who you are, where you are, and why you are the way you are. This enables growth. Anything that is not growing is dead. Death is the only case where it would be okay to ignore your soul.

— CONNECTING WITH THE SOUL —

Are you alive?

Is the argument between your heart and mind stopping you from hearing your soul?

Have you ever believed something in your soul that your heart didn't feel and/or your mind did not think?

Which one did you go with?

What would your life be like if you had listened to each one of the other two?

Discuss today's topic with other readers at
www.solitary-refinement.com.

A challenge from the Author:
Our soul is more valuable than our heart, mind,
or anything else we could ever possess.

For what will it profit a man if he gains the whole world and forfeits his soul? Or what will a man give in exchange for his soul? *~Matthew 16:26 (NASB)*

STOP Remember …

Read, meditate, and process just one day at a time.

Don't rush your journey.

DAY 22: Lies in the Mind vs. Truth in the Soul

About a year before high school, I attended an elementary school with a program for disabled students, much like the special school I attended the year before. I spent the whole day in one classroom called "Resource." One day, while I was talking to one of my classmates, I happened to mention my dream of going to college. The Resource teacher overheard me and corrected me on this. She said that, at best, I might go to trade school. But, college was not in the plans for me. For some reason, that just didn't faze me. Yes, I thought about it. I thought about it a lot. But, there was something in me that had already confirmed that I would go to college and live a productive life. At that point, my condition demonstrated evidence that I was living in denial. However, today I am a college graduate.

You are who you are, without social injustice and before the trials of life. Wait! Think about that and give it time to resonate. The peak of our existence is not defined by our career, personal likes and dislikes, opinions, achievements, awards, or acknowledgements. Rather, it is defined by the declaration of truth in our soul.

We all have a level of hope, belief and faith in ourselves deep down inside. All of us look forward to doing what we know we can do. No one can stop man from dreaming. We all find assurance in the potential of something or someone.

You can consciously convince yourself that a fantasy can be your identity.

Every boy and girl has unlimited possibilities. Each man and woman has the capability of being worthy of love. We know that everyone is teachable. You and I can add more to our life and the lives of those who surround us.

So, what went wrong? Very few people are in an environment in which they can thrive. Our minds were polluted. Some of us grew up thinking that money or power defines who we are. We were told that no matter what we believe, we cannot achieve it because the world belongs to a certain ethnic group or people of certain financial levels. Or our mental abilities are not sufficient for the life we desire. Someone who does not value their own life has tried to devalue yours by telling you, "You will never be worth nothing." Yes, that is improper English. So, why are you listening to them in the first place?

Guess what? Not every lie that enters your mind comes from an outside source. You have lied to yourself. *You can consciously convince yourself that a fantasy can be your identity.* How can I put this: Those pants do not fit. Stop deluding yourself. Take them back to the store. You laugh, but you know where I'm coming from, do you not? The pants do not need alteration; you do.

Now that we have that straightened out, let's move on. It is too painful to live with truth in our souls and a lie in our minds. The technical term for this is simple-interconflict. Your mind and soul want to achieve something but can't without preventing the other from doing so. They are in a tug-of-war with each other. You see, in the middle of your mind and soul is the heart of who you are. The lies in your mind are pulling your heart one direction, while the truth in your soul is pulling it in the other direction. I am sad to say, this is where most of us live. We are living with a broken heart because of the lies that fight against the truth.

EMERGENCY SURGERY

It is time to plant a Truth Filter in your life. This is a strainer on the heart, mind, and soul that separates facts from opinions. I know I have talked about this in previous days, but today is different. Today will require an implant. The surgery is just as critical and intense as a simultaneous brain and heart surgery. This surgery will forever change the soul that is within you. Once the filter is in place, it will become a crucial part of you. Like any other transplant of this nature, once it is done it's done … and if you reject it, you will die on the inside.

Why is this procedure necessary? When a person faces truth and confronts lies, they put a spotlight on their flaws. Those flaws trigger insecurities. Those insecurities press the button that opens the door for external lies to come in. External lies are the thoughts, opinions, and judgments we allow to affect our hearts, minds, and souls without going through the Truth Filter. These thoughts, opinions, and judgments are many times coming from people with their own flaws, insecurities, and external lies; therein lies the problem. Please hear me clearly on this. I am not saying that your family and friends or I would intentionally lead you astray. I'm saying we are not perfect; therefore, you must have a method to single out fact from fiction. If this transplant is successful, you will be able to confess, correct, and confront lies and truths in your life.

—— CONNECTING WITH THE SOUL ——

Not confessing the issues, correcting the mistakes, and confronting the truth of your life leaves the door open for a lie.

Step 1 - Confess: Bring everything to the surface. Tell yourself and three of your closest friends what you know to be true and false about the issues.

Step 2 - Correct: Remove the errors. Make any changes needed to eliminate the power that the false action has on the situation.

Step 3 - Confront: Uncover and come to the crossroads of facts. Honestly have an encounter with the truth, whether positive or negative.

Discuss today's topic with other readers at
www.solitary-refinement.com.

A challenge from the Author:
The Bible is truth for our soul.

All Scripture is inspired by God and profitable for teaching,
for reproof, for correction, for training in righteousness;
so that the man of God may be adequate, equipped for
every good work. ~2 Timothy 3:16-17

STOP Remember …

Read, meditate, and process just one day at a time.

Don't rush your journey.

DAY 23: Broken Dreams

I would say nine out of every ten of my friends share with me a dream they had of me walking. Every time, I think they are surprised with my response. I don't show excitement or even hope. I'm just interested in what they are saying. Somebody asked me one day, "Do you even want to walk?" To be truthful, this was my dream most of my childhood. I really built my life around the idea of one day walking. But, about midway through high school, I started to accept that this dream of mine may not become a reality. Not only that, but I started to believe there may be a purpose for my disability. Today, I have traveled all over the country motivating and challenging people to live a life outside of their circumstances. I can truly say that when I accepted the broken dream for my life, I found real purpose and meaning in my disability.

Man can follow a dream or pursue his destiny. Sadly, in today's world, we oftentimes chase the dream long before we hunt for our destiny. Dreams, whether broken or fulfilled, tell you a lot about who you are and who you are destined to be. People who choose to live their lives in reality probably have more broken dreams than fulfilled ones. The interpretations of the broken dreams can be the most informative resources in your life.

It is the reality of your broken dreams that reveals your true purpose.

Dreams are fantasies, ideas, emotions, and images in your mind. They are temporary, with no real substance. Purpose is the concentrated nature of who you are. It is what you get when you stop defining yourself by financial status, social environment, education level, mistakes, let downs, unfortunate circumstances, and misfortune.

Dreams can cheat us out of our destiny. If you have not had a broken dream, it is likely that you are not fulfilling your purpose. Broken dreams pull us out of the fantasy world and into reality. A life without broken dreams is a life of fantasies with no meaning and no direction. Broken dreams give us something to really strive for in life. Broken dreams lift us from the commonplace and bring us to a place of purpose. *It is the reality of your broken dreams that reveals your true purpose.*

TOO MUCH HOT AIR

Purpose is whatever makes you value your life. It is the answer to the question, "Why me?" The person that seems unbalanced has not yet found their purpose. Your purpose is your traction in an unstable life. Something of this magnitude in your life is like air to a balloon. When you put air into a balloon, it starts to stretch. Then there comes a point where the balloon cannot expand anymore, causing it to burst. Your dreams are only a balloon. There is only so much purpose it can contain.

To get our heads around the concept of finding our purpose through our broken dreams, I have two scenarios to present to you. The first is the man who has the dream of being married for the rest of his life to the woman who will always be a perfect size six. After two kids, the process of pregnancy and birth shatters the dream for him. His perfect size six is no longer a reasonable goal. However, his wife's dedication to motherhood and commitment to her marriage is obvious. Now he sees in her a woman to be valued and respected. His dream was to have the perpetual trophy wife, but his purpose is to become the type of husband that can appreciate, love and respect a lady of her caliber. Who she is as a mother and wife could never fit in a size six.

The second scenario is the woman who had the dream of a perfect marriage and a house with a white picket fence. Over time, her dreams are shattered by an uncommitted husband and a deadbeat father. Yet, she still has the responsibility of raising a child to become a responsible and contributing adult. She cannot allow the spouse that left the scene to deter her from being the type of parent her child needs. Her dream was to be a wife, but her purpose is motherhood. The white picket fence can no longer fit around the purpose for her life.

In both scenarios, we can see how broken dreams can expose the true purpose of one's life. This dream that you have been chasing and trying to seal back together must eventually come loose and be broken for your purpose to be discovered. Let me clear up something here. These scenarios are not about showing you that I have compassion. Rather, it is about revealing how shallow we can be. Who finds purpose in a white picket fence or a perfect size six? We look for purpose outside of ourselves because we fear we are too shallow to contain it within us. We are living in a dream world if we seek to find our purpose in someone else.

Many times, we try to contain all of our purpose within a dream. It simply cannot be done. Fulfilled purpose is an exploded dream. Those cracks in the plan allow us to look beneath the surface of our lives. There we will discover a purpose that is bigger than our dream.

—— CONNECTING WITH THE SOUL ——

What are your broken dreams?

What are the pros and cons of your broken dreams?

How would your life be different if every dream were fulfilled?

Do you know your purpose in life?

What dream could have contained your purpose?

Discuss today's topic with other readers at
www.solitary-refinement.com.

A challenge from the Author:
God wants you to come out of dreamland and
realize His purpose for your life.

Now to Him who is able to do far more abundantly beyond all that we ask or think, according to the power that works within us... ~Ephesians 3:20 (NASB)

 Remember ...

Read, meditate, and process just one day at a time.

Don't rush your journey.

DAY 24: Your Life is Not Over

Some of us have been through a lot. We have seen and experienced more than the average person goes through in a lifetime. Then there are others who have awakened from a sickness or an accident that is preventing them from doing what they were be able to do before. In both cases, you are tired. You are ready for everything to come to an end. Mentally, you have put yourself in the corner of life and you're just waiting for your time to come. If your eyes popped open this morning, it was for a reason. Whether you like it or not, your life is not over. There is still a purpose and a meaning behind every second you are given the opportunity to live.

The problem is we don't understand the purpose behind our existence. To not understand our assignment in life is to be confused. As a result, we have animosity toward ourselves and each other. When we don't understand our individual purpose, we are compelled to live outside of our roles and area of influence. We are never able to see the significance of our lives.

Someone needs you to be who you are. You may be saying to yourself, "Yes, Chris, but I'm in this wheelchair," or "I'm in this bed and I can't move," or "I need someone to take care of me. I need someone to do everything for me. My life is a hindrance to them. My life is an inconvenience to that nurse that takes care of me everyday. My life is an inconvenience to my brother, sister, mama that has to come in and feed me everyday." And I say to you... I've been there. I've often thought the same thing, too. I've often thought that my sibling's, mother's, and father's lives would be so much better if I just hadn't been born. They had to feed me, dress me, and change my dirty clothes at 15 years of age. But now, looking back, I realize that my life was part of their purpose. My life and my dependency on them gave them purpose and meaning at that time. That was what they were there for. I was in my condition to put purpose in their lives, and that was my purpose.

YOU ARE THE PURPOSE

It's also about, facing the fact that you are alive for a reason. Maybe that person that is taking care of you needs to take care of you. Maybe you help her to see that she should not take her life for granted. Maybe you help her to show love in a way that she would never be able to show otherwise. Maybe you are helping her kids to see that life is not just about taking care of yourself. You can find purpose in your circumstances. *In your worst state of being, purpose can be found.* I personally believe that every day that the God of the universe has not chosen to release me from this life and these circumstances is because my purpose is not yet complete.

Perhaps you don't have a physical disability or some type of ailment, but you are lonely and hoping that this life will end as soon as tomorrow or tonight. The problem is that you don't have someone to take care of. You don't have someone to pour into. Everybody has a mind to change, a heart to reach, and a life to touch by just being who they are. Our lives are not about us. Too many people are trying to find purpose outside of their circumstances. We have to accept that in every circumstance lies our purpose. Therefore, circumstances will not change until that purpose is fulfilled. It is at that time, a deeper purpose is assigned.

In your worst state of being, purpose can be found.

I have to be real with you: on a planet with millions and millions of people, someone needs you, too. Someone needs your love; someone needs you to reach outside your loneliness and touch his or her life. That may be your purpose.

—— CONNECTING WITH THE SOUL ——

I don't know enough about your circumstances to ask you questions in order to lead you to your purpose. But I'm here to tell you that if someone sees you smile in your condition, you have found purpose. If someone hears you say "thank you" in your circumstances, you will change their life. You will touch their heart. You will make a difference in their life. Why can't your purpose be as simple as that? Why can't that be enough to live for?

Discuss today's topic with other readers at
www.solitary-refinement.com.

A challenge from the Author:
From my wheelchair, I would like to share with you my favorite Bible verse.

As He passed by, He saw a man blind from birth.
And His disciples asked Him, "Rabbi, who sinned,
this man or his parents, that he would be born blind?"
Jesus answered, "It was neither that this man sinned, nor
his parents; but it was so that the works of God might be
displayed in him." ~ John 9:1-3 (NASB)

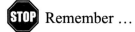 Remember ...

Read, meditate, and process just one day at a time.

Don't rush your journey.

DAY 25: The War of Forgiveness

We are trying to find freedom in our minds while embracing captivity in our souls. We let our own faults, other people's mistakes, and misunderstandings inhabit who we are. The keyword here is "harbor". We let these things come up, park, and even rest on the dock of our soul. Allowing malice to reside inside is harmful to you and everyone around you, even those you do not intend to hurt.

We think by holding a grudge we have a weapon in the war we wage against one another. In war, there are two kinds of troops. There are frontline troops. These troops are our knowledge, character, and zeal. Then there are backline troops: peace, joy, and a state of contentment. Going into battle with frontline troops can only damage our pride. Danger comes into play when the war goes on for so long that the backline troops are exposed. Our peace, joy, and state of contentment are now at risk. Our knowledge, character, and zeal have been overtaken by grudge.

WAVE THE WHITE FLAG

At some point, you have to know when to retreat. You probably think that to retreat means to give up. It really means "to withdraw yourself from difficulty and danger." Not understanding this true definition will eventually annihilate you. And though you may have a lot of frontline troops in your battalion, you don't want to take the chance of annihilating your backline troops. Why would you compromise these troops? *Your peace, joy, and state of contentment are worth retreating over.*

We all need to hear, "I forgive you." Do not let pride eat you alive. You know your heart is longing for forgiveness. You will not ask because the other person may reject you and chew your hinny out. That very well could be the case.

Nevertheless, hang in there; listen and acknowledge your wrongdoing. If you sincerely ask for forgiveness and that person decides to hold a grudge, the right to be relinquished is no longer in their hands. Even though that person has not forgiven you, the weight of unforgiveness is off of you. You can begin to heal. The truth is that, until you ask for forgiveness, you won't allow yourself to be free from the pain inside of you.

Your peace, joy, and state of contentment are worth retreating over.

I oftentimes talk about things that have happened to me and issues that have occurred in my life as a result of someone else. You know, I, too, need forgiveness. I have hurt many people. I, too, have lied, cheated, and even stolen from someone at some point in my life. Though I have not stolen anything physically, I have taken a lot from people emotionally. I hope they will forgive me, not just so I can be free, but so we all can be free. I have come to grips with the fact that as long as they have not forgiven me, I am still robbing them. Though they have made the choice not to forgive, the responsibility of my actions still plays a role in their lives. If you, whom I have hurt, are reading this book, I plead with you not to let me continue to rob you. I want freedom for both of us. I am throwing in the towel; will you? There are things that will not let go of you until you let go of them.

—— CONNECTING WITH THE SOUL ——

Have you truly chosen to let bygones be bygones?

Who are you allowing to rob you by not forgiving them?

Who do you need to ask for forgiveness?

Truthfully, how has this issue of forgiveness affected the people around you?

Discuss today's topic with other readers at
www.solitary-refinement.com.

A challenge from the Author:
People have waged a war against God who has
the right and power to annihilate us,
but He has retreated so we can have
peace, joy, and contentment.

Therefore there is now no condemnation for those who are
in Christ Jesus. For the law of the Spirit of life in Christ
Jesus has set you free from the law of sin and death.
~Romans 8:1-2 (NASB)

STOP Remember …
Read, meditate, and process just one day at a time.
Don't rush your journey.

DAY 26: Conquering vs. Surviving

Until this point in my life, most people don't know what I am about to share in this book: I am in constant pain every day, and the pain is increased by frequent seizures. The truth is most people don't know about that because I decided not to just be a survivor. You see, when I wake up from a seizure, I have survived. When I just wake up and get dressed in the morning, I have survived my pain. The fact is, beyond my situation there is a whole world out there for me to experience. There are people out there for me to love and encourage, and for them to be a part of my life. For this to happen, I cannot just be a survivor. I have to conquer my disability. I have to conquer my seizures and my pain. I have to go beyond just surviving in order for me to enjoy the life that I have been given. Some people never enjoy their lives because they never move from their survival mode to becoming a conqueror. They just want to make it to one more day. But, I am here to tell you that real enjoyment, no matter what your situation, is when you decide to conquer that situation.

Life will try you. It will not back down. It will put

you through test after test after test after test. However, if you pay close attention, you will see many of these tests are over the same material, just in a different format. Why? Because we take these tests with a survival mentality. We just want to do enough to remain alive through it all.

I said it before and I'll say it again: "Animals survive; people conquer." Many times when adversity enters our lives, we get bogged down with the situation at hand. This distraction stops us from gathering the firepower we need to dogmatically attack life's tests. Let us not get wrapped up in a big pity party. This is the time we have to pull ourselves together, find strength from deep down within, and concentrate on the problem at hand.

Hardships will occur in your life. There is no way to go over them, get around them, or go under them. You must go through them. Now you ask, "Are you saying I should anticipate a time of distress?" What I'm saying here is, preparing for the after-effects of life's challenges is one of the keys to overcoming. We have to know what needs to be done when the trials come our way.

CONQUERORS DO NOT COMPROMISE

With this in mind, you must understand that

preparation is the foundation for the rest of your life. When a builder builds a home, the first thing they do is carefully set the foundation because they realize the foundation will be there for the lifespan of the home. Part of conquering and not just surviving in life is laying down a foundation so that it does not matter what happens in life; this is who you are. *A person that is set on conquering something will compromise nothing.* You will never be tomorrow what you are not preparing to be today.

Survival means that you will be temporarily happy under the right conditions, whereas conquering means that you will experience joy under any circumstances. Many people only survive in this life because they rely on excuses not to fight back. Their condition is their reason to stay where they are. To be honest, many people do not want to rise above it because they like having the excuse for not having to do something about it.

A person that is set on conquering something will compromise nothing.

Conquering life's trials means to diligently search for an opportunity for your life to be enhanced when it's all said and done. There is an opportunity in every obstacle. Therefore, you must face the obstacle in pursuit of a real opportunity to bring yourself to a higher level. The ordeals of life are to be used to help you grow spiritually, physically, and emotionally.

Let's face it; sometimes adversities come as a result of incorrect attitudes and actions of the mind, heart, and soul. The correction of these attitudes and actions is what allows us to face and conquer adversities. Many people blame themselves for the conditions that they are in. And that is all they do. They say it is my fault for this and my fault for that. Sounds good. They are accepting their mistakes. But my question would be, "When will you correct those mistakes?"

There is a difference between taking blame and taking responsibility. Taking blame for something and not making a change in your life does no good. You have to come to the point where you say to yourself that it is time to do something about your situation. You must yourself, "How badly do I want it?" When you want something badly enough, you do not wait around for someone else to take responsibility for it.

Every test in life will ask, "What will it take to master the situation?" In order to become a conqueror, you must defeat something in your life. Until you overcome, life will continue to put you through the same old test. Everybody at some point has to stop eating off the silver platter of life and face life head on. You have to do what it takes to master the situation. Conquering and not just surviving requires going through adversities and coming back a better person because of them.

—— CONNECTING WITH THE SOUL ——

What makes this situation a challenge?

What will it take for you to survive?

What would it take for you to conquer?

Why would you choose one over the other?

Discuss today's topic with other readers at
www.solitary-refinement.com.

**A challenge from the Author:
Grabbing hold of the love of God is the
secret to conquering life.**

*Just as it is written, "For Your sake we are being put to
death all day long; we were considered as sheep to be
slaughtered." But in all these things we overwhelmingly
conquer through Him who loved us.*
~Romans 8:36-37 (NASB)

 Remember …
Read, meditate, and process just one day at a time.
Don't rush your journey.

DAY 27: Self-Inflicted Bondage

Many times, when I am in a public place, I get the blank stare, the child that says, "Mommy, he sounds funny," or the people who choose not to acknowledge my existence. For a long time, this bothered me. Eventually, I started to believe that no one would ever truly see me as the person I am. This thought imprisoned me for a time in my life. Midway through college, I started to meet well-rounded and open-minded individuals. These people truly wanted to see beyond my wheelchair. However, I was so used to putting up my protective shield that it prevented them from getting in. Ironically, I could not get out. What I used to protect myself ended up being my invisible, self-inflicted bondage.

The most difficult chains to unlock or break are the invisible ones. Our imagination can link us to walls that are not there and poles that have been removed. Until you spot the invisible chains, you are a slave to yourself. Whatever makes you act, think, or feel like a victim is bondage. However, what you think and feel is oftentimes not the case; therefore, your actions are not justified. These types of clutches on our lives are invisible, self-inflicted chains.

When you refuse to give your soul the freedom it longs for, you are bound to find yourself in a civil war that you cannot win. Two sides with equal amounts of power will only annihilate each other. It is called self-destruction. Either you have to allow yourself to be free, or you will destroy yourself.

When was the most dangerous time for a slave? Contrary to popular belief, it wasn't when they traveled from the South to the North using the Underground Railroad. True, they did run the risk of being killed on that journey. However, there was a more dangerous time than that. The most dangerous time was when the slaves themselves accepted the fact that they were slaves. This self-inflicted bondage will not kill you, but it will put you into a comatose state. You end up in a state of mind in which you do not pursue hope in anything beyond the present condition. At that time, you become your own slave-master, mentally. Your body is now the plantation home that keeps your mind, heart, and soul imprisoned.

THE RESPONSIBILITY OF FREEDOM

Many slaves did not desire to obtain freedom simply because they did not know what they would do with it. The idea of being free was a fearful thought for them. All they had ever known was in the confines of being a slave. I hate to say it, but *our self-inflicted bondage may be a result of the fear of being free.* We do not know what we would do if we did not have a reason to live the way we are living. We are afraid that we cannot live up to the responsibility of freedom. The reality of freedom enables us to liberate ourselves. Freedom requires you to accept that you have no one to blame and there are no excuses. No longer having anyone to blame, and no excuses to rely on, would force us to find our own path.

Our self-inflicted bondage may be a result of the fear of being free.

Some people don't run for freedom because they are prepared to only go a certain distance. Taking hold of the baton of liberty requires us to go a lot further than we are sometimes willing to go. We think our pathway to freedom should be short and sweet. If it isn't, we stop and wait for someone else to show us the way or we just continue to play the victim role.

It is easier to retreat as a victim than it is to fight for victory. When you choose to retreat rather than fight for freedom, you become a part of the slave trade. The very moment you give up on your freedom, your bondage is self-inflicted. The key to unlocking invisible, self inflicted chains is to bind yourself to what is real and true. The worst type of slave owner is the one that holds themselves in bondage. They feel so incapable of being equal to another human being, that they cannot recognize the Underground Railroad within themselves. They cannot see that the pathway to freedom is found within their own heart, mind, and soul.

—— CONNECTING WITH THE SOUL ——

What is your definition of freedom?

What in you contradicts your definition of freedom?

What is stopping you from using the Underground Railroad within yourself?

What is real and true in your life?

Discuss today's topic with other readers at
www.solitary-refinement.com.

A challenge from the Author:
Freedom is the privilege of praising God in the
midst of the walls around you that you have
labeled as bondage.

But about midnight Paul and Silas were praying and
singing hymns of praise to God, and the prisoners were
listening to them... ~Acts 16:25 (NASB)

 Remember ...
Read, meditate, and process just one day at a time.
Don't rush your journey.

DAY 28: Cultivating a Significant Life

I cannot deny it. My family played a very valuable and crucial role in my life. They made sure that I had everything that could be given to me in order for me to live a productive life. As a result, I took it and ran with it, reaching heights that even I never thought I would reach. Now, I believe some members of my family think that I feel that I am better than them due to my education, extensive travel, and the people I attract. They are right; I do want to be better, but not better than them; better than myself. Everyday I have to look out into the fields of my life and ask, "What can I do to grow today?"

Our parents cultivated our lives when we were younger. They did whatever they could do to help develop and prepare us for life. Some of you may say, "My parents did nothing. They could not have cared less." I am sorry for that. But, get over it. At this point, you are responsible for your life, not them.

Now, a significant life must be cultivated. Once we reach adulthood, we run a greater risk of neglect. You and

I cannot just go wild from here on out. When mistakes and bad decisions pop up in life, we often fail to pull them out before they take root. Our lives grow full of weeds and become useless through neglect. This becomes a futile life; a life that is incapable of producing any results. It is your responsibility to guard, enhance, and monitor your development. Mommy and Daddy can't do that for you. Are you cultivating your life?

An unguarded life leads to unnecessary wars in life. To guard your life, you must have a vision. A vision is a shield of protection in one's life. A person with no vision for their life has not found their reason for living and is open for anything. Other people's ideals and perspectives will come in and try to take over. A guaranteed way to go down the wrong path is to follow someone else's path. Your vision will keep you on your path. It will keep you focused on the end result.

The best way to enhance your life is to set goals. Always ask yourself questions like, "What can I add to my job, family, marriage, and relationships with others? What is next in this life for me?" Keep in mind that there will always be things you need to accomplish that will add to who you are. When you get bogged down with life, your goals will immediately grab your attention and say, "Hold up. Let us not forget what is really important here."

FAILURE IS NOT AN OPTION

A mission monitors the development of your life. It holds you accountable and does not let you contradict yourself. Without a mission, your vision and goals will never be achieved. It is crucial to understand your mission because it is what makes your life significant. The hardest thing to understand about a mission is that it is never assigned for the benefit of one person. With this in mind let me tell you, as people, we have to be careful about what we define as a life of significance. A life of significance is a life that has positively affected someone else's life. Your mission in life, no matter who you are, is to play a significant role in someone's life. *If your husband, your wife, your mother, your father, your boyfriend, your girlfriend, your best friend, or your*

If your husband, your wife, your mother, your father, your boyfriend, your girlfriend, your best friend, or your child has not been positively affected through a relationship with you, your life is insignificant.

child has not been positively affected through a relationship with you, your life is insignificant. You have failed at your mission, your vision is meaningless, and your goals are weak attempts to fill a void.

A person with a failed mission, meaningless vision, and an empty life is a selfish and lazy person. You need to know that living a life of significance requires you to stop being paralyzed by the consequences and do something significant for someone other than yourself. When trying to do something significant with your life, consequences are irrelevant.

—— CONNECTING WITH THE SOUL ——

What are your vision and goals in life?

Have you expected your mission to play a role of significance in all of your relationships?

Are you willing to face the consequences of becoming that person?

Discuss today's topic with other readers at
www.solitary-refinement.com.

A challenge from the Author
God is prepared to help you deal with the
consequences of doing great things with your life.

'For I know the plans that I have for you,' declares the Lord,
'plans for welfare and not for calamity to give you a future
and a hope.' ~Jeremiah 29:11 (NASB)

> **STOP** Remember …
> Read, meditate, and process just one day at a time.
> Don't rush your journey.

DAY 29: Moments of Hopelessness

Before you skip this day and say to yourself, "Never for a moment have I had that thought," let me just say that you are either lying to yourself or you have not lived long enough. Life will eventually back us all into a small, dark corner, unprepared or unwilling to fight back. In those moments, we all have thoughts of giving up. You may get a little bit defensive and even say, "I am a Christian. I will never think like that." However, God Himself tells us all to "choose life" as if there will come a time in life that giving up will be an option. We all have to face moments of hopelessness. Circumstances of life do get out of our control. For many, not dealing with these moments results in emotional suicide.

It is true; some of us will never physically harm ourselves, but emotionally we are dying to check out. The substance industry is supported by people who have emotionally committed suicide. Our psychiatric wards are full of people who have mentally given up on life. So don't kid yourself when you say, "This is not an issue I face for one second."

Four months before the time of writing on this

subject, I lost a very dear and close friend of mine to suicide. Unbeknownst to me and the majority of his friends, he suffered from bipolar disorder. And though I understand the nature of this horrible disease, I can't help but ask myself, "Why didn't he talk to me?" Of all the people that would have understood where he was coming from, it would have been me. No, I'm not blaming myself for his decision. But I often wonder if my friend had fully considered the reality of what he was about to do.

LOVE IS A LIGHT

I wish he would have given me a chance to talk to him about two realities of life. The first reality is, someone cares. It may not be the people you want to care. Your mother, father, husband or wife may not care. But on this planet of billions of people, someone will love you for who you are. There is someone in an even deeper and darker corner that needs you to show them the light. Don't get me wrong; his mom, dad, brother, and friends cared about him deeply. But at that page in his life, he thought that hopelessness overshadowed that love. I just wanted to tell him that the light of love can never be overshadowed by any amount of darkness.

The second reality that I wish he had been able to see

is that God loves him. Now, some of my readers are turned off by me throwing God into the equation. But I want to ask you to do me a favor. If what you have read has brought you this far in your journey, then at least hear me out. Not believing in God is the core of hopelessness. We can solve all the problems of the world, but there will still be one issue we cannot fix. That issue is death. No one on earth can set back the timer on life, and life has to be in someone's hands. If we can't believe in that, what can we believe in? *If there's no hope in the fact that someone controls the universe, then life, no matter what you do with it, is hopeless.*

If there's no hope in the fact that someone controls the universe, then life, no matter what you do with it, is hopeless.

A few days before writing this chapter, a friend of mine gave me a CD and told me one of the songs would become one of my favorites. He was right. The lyrics of this song by Rita Springer go like this:

I have to believe that He sees my darkness.
I have to believe that God sees the moments in my life when

I'm not shining to my full potential.

I have to believe that He knows my pain.

Thirty-four years of cerebral palsy have torn down my joints and ligaments. For the last six years, I have been in constant pain. My pain will never decrease, but will always increase every year I am alive. I believe He knows the pain I am in and His mercy and grace will sustain me.

I have to lift up my hands to worship His name.

I believe that my purpose for living, even in my condition, is to worship Him.

I have to declare that He is my refuge.

There's no doubt about it; I find comfort and a safe place of knowing and believing in Jesus.

I have to deny that I am alone.

I feel the presence of God with me each day of my life. I am among a lot of people who do not understand the difficulties of a disabled life, but I'm not alone.

I have to lift up my eyes to the mountains, where my help comes from.

I know all the success I have experienced in my life, in spite of my disability, has come from God.

I have to stand tall when the wind blows me over.

Day after day, I face adversities that this life brings me, but I will not back down from living the life I know God gave me. *I have to stand strong when I'm weak and afraid.*

I cannot tell you how many times since I've moved to Georgia that I have found myself weak and afraid. Many times, I didn't know how I was going to get to the next day, but I couldn't stop; I had to press on. Something in me would not let me let go. There were many nights that I sang and praised my way out of the dark and cold corners of my life. Because of my belief in Him, my chains that confine me to my wheelchair have been broken. I have found freedom in a life of captivity. There is no hopeless situation when your faith is in God.

—— CONNECTING WITH THE SOUL ——

What is your dark corner?

What unbelief has convinced you that life is hopeless?

Why can't you run to God for refuge?

If the God I believe in can move my mountains, why can't He move yours?

Discuss today's topic with other readers at
www.solitary-refinement.com.

A challenge from the Author:
If you really look with your heart and soul for something more to this life, you will find it.

But from there you will seek the Lord your God, and you will find Him if you search for Him with all your heart and all your soul. ~ Deuteronomy 4:29 (NASB)

STOP Remember …
Read, meditate, and process just one day at a time.
Don't rush your journey.

DAY 30: Mercy and Grace

The purpose of this journey we have been on is to get you to this place by focusing on all of the issues in your life. Now that we are here, let me tell you that you can read all the books and do all the different exercises to make yourself a better person and it will still not be enough. There will always be something in your life that you cannot fix. There will always be issues you don't have the ability to correct. A positive attitude, this book, and all of the psychologists in the world cannot fix you and me. Somewhere out there, there has to be a remedy for our sickness, a remedy for internal illness.

I don't know about you, but this human, this body, this flesh will always find a way to do wrong, no matter how hard I try to do good. I've found the remedy in my life to be mercy and grace. Do not draw back from this book now.

If the world had to survive without mercy or grace, the human race would quickly become extinct.

For the last 29 days, I intentionally tried not to approach

things from a spiritual standpoint. I think I have done well. However, as the author, I feel that if you are not at the point where you see a need for mercy and grace in your life, I have failed you. I would like to believe you cannot process the last 29 days of your life and not see the need there. The fact is, *if the world had to survive without mercy or grace, the human race would quickly become extinct.* There would be no room for second chances, rehabilitation, forgiveness, or even judgment. Judgment itself requires a chance to be proven guilty or not guilty. Without mercy and grace, every action would be immediately condemned.

During this time, I am sure we have all thought of some unforgivable things we have done; things we would never tell another we did, much less ask for forgiveness. Have you ever come to the point in your life where you are amazed by your own actions? Where you shake your head at the thought of what you have done? Can you think of a point in your life where you cannot forgive yourself? Do you look up at the walls of your life and wonder why they aren't falling in on top of you? Well that, my friends, is mercy and grace. That is mercy and grace holding the walls of your life up, keeping them from crashing down on you.

WHO WILL PLEAD YOUR CASE?

Even though mercy and grace are often lumped together, they are definitely two different entities of life. They are twins, but not identical, by any means. Now, I have to be careful here and let you know that mercy and grace do not erase the consequences; they lessen the consequences. They are lawyers in your life that plead your case, knowing that you are guilty. Knowing that there is going to be some type of repercussion, they plead that you do not get your full sentence for what you have done.

Let's talk a little about grace. Grace is spiritual release from the bondage of the world. It helps us carry the burdens that life imposes on us. Receiving grace is very much like water is to a plant; it causes growth. It gives the power to move forward in the midst of sorrow for your mistakes. God established grace with the understanding that we will all need it, and it is a very essential characteristic of who He is.

If you want to put love to the test, bring up something that requires mercy. Mercy is not allowing what should be done, to be done. It is forgiveness taken to the highest level. Mercy is forgiveness for the unforgivable. Suppose for a moment that heaven is real and there will be someone standing there looking over your whole life to decide where you will spend eternity. Do you not need mercy? God knows we will.

Here's what I believe. I believe that one day I will find myself in the public eye. And in the public eye, there will be room for the media to scrutinize me. When they look back over my lifetime, they will find moments of "oops," moments of "uh-oh," moments of "I wish I hadn't done that," moments that cannot be forgiven by any person, no matter how much they love me, moments that can only be redeemed by the Redeemer himself, Jesus Christ. Due to this fact, when the time comes that someone will look at me with disappointment and shame, I take comfort in knowing that my refuge is found in Jesus Christ and Jesus Christ alone. The forgiveness my heart will long for will be found in who I know God to be. Some may call this religion, some may call this stupidity, some may call it brainwashing, some may even call it weak-minded. You can call it whatever you want, but the bottom line is I have spent my whole life in difficult circumstances with a smile on my face 95% of the time. I call it hope. I call it freedom. I call it healing. I call it mercy and grace that no man can offer. It is divine forgiveness.

Think about your life. Think about all the things that you have done. Think about the things that no one else knows about you. Are you prepared for the full sentence? Are you prepared to truly reap what you have sown? Can you live without mercy? That is what I am asking you today. Every day of my life, I have to wake up and say, "Lord, have mercy on me." When the doctor says, "There is no way," we need mercy. When the judge says, "This is your sentence," we need mercy. When life comes at us with all that it has, we need mercy.

—— CONNECTING WITH THE SOUL ——

Where does your hope come from?

When man cannot forgive, where do you find comfort for your heart and soul?

Where is your mercy?

Where is your grace?

Do you have someone that you can run to that guarantees you forgiveness no matter what?

Discuss today's topic with other readers at
www.solitary-refinement.com.

A challenge from the Author:
The grace and mercy of God belongs to
anyone who will take hold of it.

For we do not have a high priest who cannot sympathize
with our weaknesses, but One who has been tempted in
all things as we are, yet without sin. Therefore let us draw
near with confidence to the throne of grace, so that we may
receive mercy and find grace to help in time of need.
~Hebrews 4:15-16 (NASB)

 Remember ...
Read, meditate, and process just one day at a time.
Don't rush your journey.

DAY 31: Don't Turn Out the Light and Shut the Door

As I get closer to finishing this book, my heart gets a little bit tighter. I know that publishing it will require me to practice what I preach. You now have a right to hold me accountable to the challenges I have given you for your life. And that is only fair; wouldn't you say?

Ok, then. Freeze! The final step on this journey is between two landmines. The next move could cause everything you have been working for to blow up in your face. There is a very good chance when you shut this book, you will disregard all you have learned. That, my friend, would be the wrong move.

The hardest part of discovering something about yourself is accepting it. Our natural response is to resist the knowledge of it. To be truthful, some of this you knew about from the very beginning, but tried not to deal with it. You did not realize that the time you spent in this journal would uncover those issues and force you to revisit the fractured places. It is important not to go into shock at this stage. You must hold yourself together and see what the light is exposing.

We shined a light in the dark places of your life, not to reveal the issues, but to remove them. If they are lurking around in the darkness, it's because they do not belong there.

You must be willing to raise the stakes and deal with who you are. It doesn't matter what you have done. It doesn't matter what you plan on doing. In order to see tomorrow, you must pay the price of today. *You now have to become so forceful that a separation is driven between you and your issue.* If it hurts, oh well; it cannot remain in you.

Once you hear, see, or experience a character flaw in yourself, you have to answer for it. You may want to think that you are an exception to the rule, but you are not. You must decide to tear down and rebuild that section of your life. That's right, you heard me: you have to devote some time to strengthening and developing who you are. You didn't think this journal would do it all for you, did you?

> *You now have to become so forceful that a separation is driven between you and your issue.*

THE VERDICT IS IN

One of my favorite movie lines is from A Few Good

Men with Jack Nicholson and Tom Cruise. Jack Nicholson is on the witness stand and he asks Tom Cruise, "What do you want from me?" Tom Cruise answers, "I want the truth!" At that moment, Jack Nicholson lays all of his acting ability out on the table and says with so much passion and conviction this unforgettable line, "You can't handle the truth!"

That cannot be your reality. You cannot end this journal and disregard anything that has surfaced during our time together. What has been discovered and revealed over the last 30 days are the internal wheelchairs to which you allow your life to be confined. The purpose of this journey is to help you break free by facing yourself; to no longer be imprisoned by your mind, heart, and soul. You are not the victim. You are now the jury. What is your verdict: freedom or captivity?

If you chose freedom, then you must deal with the broken pieces of your life. You cannot cover them back up. What you have now is truth. If your mind has been misinformed, correct it by feeding it truth. If your heart has led you astray, confront it with the truth. If you are feeling detached from who you really are, connect with your soul by anchoring down in the truth.

Today, I am free from this wheelchair because I have faced my issues with the truth. Like me, you have to stop being afraid of what may or may not happen. Yes, it is going to be uncomfortable to get out of your wheelchair. Yes, you are going to have to face some things that you may not want to face. However, the freedom you will experience from getting out of your wheelchair will be worth the consequences.

When I decided to move to Georgia, away from my family, and declared my independence, I was aware of the consequences. I knew I was facing a challenge and there would be battles that I would lose. To be honest with you, I went through some heartbreak, pain, and struggles that I would never have had to face if I had remained in Louisiana. But by the same token, if I had focused on the consequences, I would not be the man I am today. I would have stayed confined to the wheelchair of living with the expectations that come with the label "disability." I would have continued to focus on my disability and possibly never discovered my abilities; never really knowing who God made me to be and why.

Now here you are, face-to-face with your issues. Something has to give. There has to be an altercation between your mind, heart, and soul. The outcome must be a transformation, your liberation from the inside-out.

—— CONNECTING WITH THE SOUL ——

What have you discovered about yourself in the last 31 days?

What do you have to do to deal with it?

DEAL WITH IT.

Discuss today's topic with other readers at
www.solitary-refinement.com.

A challenge from the Author:
You can trust what has been discovered to God.

…but if we walk in the Light as He Himself is in the Light,
we have fellowship with one another, and the blood of Jesus
His Son cleanses us from all sin. ~ 1 John 1:7 (NASB)

 Remember …
Read, meditate, and process just one day at a time.
Don't rush your journey.

To learn more about Christopher Coleman or
to book him for an upcoming
speaking engagement, visit
www.solitary-refinement.com